THE IMPERFECT ART

The
Imperfect
Art

REFLECTIONS ON JAZZ
AND MODERN CULTURE

TED GIOIA

New York   Oxford
OXFORD UNIVERSITY PRESS
1988

OXFORD UNIVERSITY PRESS

Oxford   New York   Toronto
Delhi   Bombay   Calcutta   Madras   Karachi
Petaling Jaya   Singapore   Hong Kong   Tokyo
Nairobi   Dar es Salaam   Cape Town
Melbourne   Auckland

and associated companies in
Beirut   Berlin   Ibadan   Nicosia

Copyright © 1988 by Ted Gioia

Published by Oxford University Press, Inc.,
200 Madison Avenue, New York, New York 10016

Oxford is a registered trademark of Oxford University Press

LIBRARY OF CONGRESS CATALOGING-IN-PUBLICATION DATA
Gioia, Ted.
The imperfect art.
Includes index.
1. Jazz music—History and criticism.
2. Music—Philosophy and aesthetics.   I. Title.
ML3506.G56   1988   785.42'09   87-34970
ISBN 0-19-505343-5

9 8 7 6 5 4 3 2 1

Printed in the United States of America
on acid-free paper

Acknowledgments

Many of the ideas that inspired this work date back to the early 1980s when I was living overseas in England. One might imagine that the academic setting of Trinity College, Oxford—where I was studying at the time—would be a conducive setting for discursive thought of any sort. But, as I look back on it, my interactions with fellow jazz musicians in the Oxford area are what stand out most in my mind, even more than my academic pursuits. My long conversations with saxophonist John O'Neill were as valuable as any tutorial or lecture in shaping my thoughts on music; and our innumerable practice sessions and (less frequent) performances were as demanding as a *viva voce* as we tried to put our ideas about jazz into practice.

I hope that the finished work retains, to some extent, the flavor of those early conversations. Although mine is a decidedly "thoughtful" (for want of a better word) approach to jazz, those expecting the relentless unfolding of a theoretical framework may well be disappointed. Jazz is a spontaneous art, and writing about it should retain some of that spontaneity. Accordingly, I have willingly pursued the occasional odd tangent, the enticing aside. Each chapter, in fact, can stand alone—as a separate conversation, if you will, or, perhaps more accurately, as a separate angle of view on my subject. I trust that, as the reader proceeds, the interaction and relations between these separate angles of vision will become more and more clear.

In the course of writing this work I benefited enormously from the input of many individuals. Among those who saw earlier versions of this work, I would like to thank the following for their comments, criticisms and/or encouragement: Richard Burgin, Robert S. Clark, Claudia Clausius, Martha Davis, Lori Dobbins, Stan Getz, Dana Gioia, Jim Harper, Howard Junker, Joseph Mailander, Miriam Miller, Frederick Morgan, Jim Nadel, Ken Oshman, Grover Sales, and Herb Wong. My thanks is also extended to the following publications in which portions of this work originally appeared: *Boulevard, Croton Review, Hudson Review,* and *Musical Quarterly.* Any defects in the present work are, of course, entirely my own.

My gratitude is also due to Fran Vella, for taking my hand-scrawled pages and transforming them into a neatly typed manuscript. Finally, I owe a special thanks to my editor at Oxford University Press, Sheldon Meyer.

Palo Alto   TG
June 1987

Contents

I   Louis Armstrong and Furniture Music, 3

II Jazz and the Primitivist Myth, 19

III The Imperfect Art, 50

IV Neoclassicism in Jazz, 70

V   What Has Jazz to Do with Aesthetics? 95

VI Boredom and Jazz, 108

VII Jazz as Song, 127

Notes, 141

Index, 148

In memory of my uncle
Theodore E. Ortez, 1927–1955,
after whom I was named.
May this work stand for all the
books on music he never had
the opportunity to write.

THE IMPERFECT ART

I

Louis Armstrong
and Furniture Music

> Mechanical reproduction of art changes the reaction of the masses toward art. The reactionary attitude toward a Picasso painting changes into the progressive reaction toward a Chaplin movie. . . . The greater the decrease in the social significance of an art form, the sharper the distinction between criticism and enjoyment by the public.
>
> WALTER BENJAMIN, "The Work of Art in the Age of Mechanical Reproduction"

I

For twenty-four-year-old Louis Armstrong, as for countless musicians before and after him, New York stood as the final challenge for an aspiring American artist. Yet it was a challenge for which he appeared to be more than adequately prepared. Through his work with the pioneering jazz band led by cornetist Joe "King" Oliver, Armstrong had gained a degree of notoriety in Chicago and in his home town New Orleans, and had participated in a series of recordings with that group which even today are admired as the purest example of New Orleans ensemble playing.

But when Armstrong first arrived in New York, in October 1924, these credentials scarcely assured him the approval of

that city's more fickle musical patrons. For most New Yorkers of that period, jazz meant *not* the exuberant sounds of
the "King" Oliver Creole Jazz Band but, rather, the relatively tamer music of the Paul Whiteman Orchestra, and
the compositions of George Gershwin, two years older than
Armstrong, whose *Rhapsody in Blue* had premiered earlier
that year. Such musical tastes could hardly be ignored by any
musician new to Manhattan: New York, then as now, served
as a barometer for the nation as a whole, not only in the
arts but in virtually every sphere of American life. Changes
there were inevitably felt across the country, both for the
better and for the worse and what passed for art in New
York soon passed for art everywhere. Similarly the prosperity
of Wall Street financiers was fairly representative of good
times in other parts of the United States just as the stock
market crash—still five years in the future—would signal the
coming of a much gloomier economic climate throughout all
of America.

But in the heady days of October 1924, the only Depression most New Yorkers felt was depression over their base-
ball team, the Giants, who had lost the World Series only
a few days earlier to the upstart Washington Senators, or
perhaps depression over finding a reliable source of alcohol,
then nominally illegal nationwide (although, according to
reliable estimates, there were 2,500 establishments violating
this law in midtown Manhattan alone). Daily conversation
revolved around the coming presidential election and the recent Democratic convention, held in New York, at which
that state's Governor, Al Smith, narrowly lost the party's
nomination. Still another topic of interest—more than ever
before—was music, which the Victrola had brought into mil-
lions of homes and which would become such a prevalent
preoccupation that later commentators would refer to this
period simply as the "Jazz Age."

Soon after his arrival Armstrong took a job—at fifty-five dollars per week—with the Fletcher Henderson band, an ensemble which over the next decade would be instrumental in shaping the role of the big band in jazz and would pave the way for the later work of artists such as Duke Ellington, Jimmie Lunceford, and Count Basie. Despite his experience with the Oliver band, Armstrong had been Henderson's second choice for the open trumpet chair, but the bandleader's top pick—the lyrical and mellow-toned trumpeter Joe Smith—was unavailable. Henderson had first come into contact with Armstrong in 1922 while in New Orleans on tour with Ethel Waters. Two years later he remembered the strong initial impression made by this young musician, and Armstrong was hired, although his relatively poor reading ability made him a less than obvious choice for a big band which performed a number of complex scores. (Another poor reader, Bix Beiderbecke—the other great cornetist of the period—was to face a similar situation several years later when he joined the Paul Whiteman Orchestra.)

Armstrong was conscientious in his attempts to overcome this limitation, and had been working on his music reading skills even before leaving New Orleans. Even so, at the time he joined Henderson he was probably the weakest reader in the band. Henderson later claimed to recall an early rehearsal at which the band was practicing a piece which featured a sudden change in dynamics from a triple forte (*fff*) to a whispering pianissimo (*pp*). When the players reached this point in the piece everyone played softly except Armstrong, who continued blowing with full force. Henderson stopped the band; "Louis," he said, "how about that *pp*?" Armstrong replied: "I thought that meant 'pound plenty.' "[1]

If Armstrong's reading ability could be faulted, few skeptics remained when he started improvising. To a man, the Henderson bandsmen were startled by the trumpeter's inspired solos and soon the newcomer's playing was adopted as a model which the rest of the group strived to emulate. A comparison of the band's recordings before and after Armstrong's stay with them reveals his powerful impact on the playing of the other soloists. Trumpeter Rex Stewart, later recalling how Armstrong had first shown up wearing an out-of-date box-back jacket, put it succinctly: "Man, after he started playin', box-back coats was the latest style."[2]

Armstrong's playing possessed a rhythmic intensity which was qualitatively different from that of the other Henderson players. Even at that early stage of his career he was playing types of syncopation that had never been employed by previous jazz musicians; in the words of jazz scholar Richard Hadlock, Armstrong was "playing more trumpet than anyone else in jazz had been able to before."[3] A recording which dates from the period immediately following Armstrong's accession to the band shows just how far the New Orlean's trumpeter had progressed. On "Shanghai Shuffle" Armstrong sets himself the most severe of rhythmic challenges: he constructs an eight-bar improvisation out of the repetition of a single note. Had another member of Henderson's band attempted the same feat, the effect would have doubtless been one of extreme monotony; but Armstrong is able to assert his powerful rhythmic sense in forging a driving solo out of the varying duration of one tone.

There is perhaps too great a tendency among commentators on jazz, even knowledgeable ones, to overstate the importance of the rhythmic element in this provocative music. Somehow the time-honored stereotype of "foot-shuffling darkies" has translated into a view of jazz which brands it as "interesting primarily for its rhythmic effects," while the harmonic and melodic approaches of its most gifted practitioners are too often overlooked. Yet Armstrong's solo on "Shanghai Shuffle" shows the element of truth underlying this generalization; it signaled that this intoxicating music called jazz, which was rising from the South to assault the virgin ears of Northern listeners, held a rhythmic power totally unlike anything that had ever surfaced before in popular music.

In the Armstrong recordings which were to follow—"Muggles," "Potato Head Blues," "Struttin' with Some Barbeque," "West End Blues," and others—we encounter a degree of artistic finesse which makes the "popular music" label seem somehow misleading. Jazz's final break with popular music still lay twenty-five years in the future, with the experimentation and elitism of the beboppers and the hipsters, but the seeds of that inevitable break were sown by Armstrong in these early recordings—sown when he first began employing rhythms which were less and less like the simple dance rhythms that have always served as the foundation for popular music.

The poet Ezra Pound, whose work for many epitomizes the concept of modernism in the arts, once sounded a cautionary note in discussing music: "Music," he wrote, "begins to atrophy when it departs too far from the dance."[4] Many counterexamples could be found to invalidate Pound's doubtful assertion, yet such a rule of thumb makes good sense when applied to the more limited realm of popular music—such music, if it is to remain popular, must stay true to dance rhythms. With jazz, an opposed sensibility prevailed: far from atrophying, the music was liberated in an important way by the gradual elimination of dance rhythms from its vocabulary. Certainly jazz contains many elements beyond the rhythmic—melodic, harmonic, and compositional devices have contributed greatly in the evolution of the music; but these, even at their best, have rarely advanced beyond what was handed down to jazz from pre-existing Western classical traditions. In contrast, the labyrinthine subdivisions of the beat, initiated by Armstrong and furthered by his musical heirs, played by far the most crucial role in delineating jazz's position as an artistic force freed from the confining bonds of mass appeal.

II

Armstrong's achievements, despite their central role in the development of jazz, seem strangely out of place when viewed in the context of his time and place. Both Armstrong's art and life reveal him as a musical romantic—a figure more in keeping with the ethos of the nineteenth century than with his own—and, accordingly, the facts of his biography take on an almost symbolic bearing. According to most sources Armstrong, like a true American folk hero, was born on the fourth of July (probably in 1900); he was raised under the most oppressive conditions: fatherless (although he later said he could recall his mother's relationship with six "step-fathers"); dressed in hand-me-downs; in frequent contact with prostitutes, hustlers, and con men; and eventually sent to the Waif's Home were he spent his adolescence. Yet he overcame these circumstances, propelled largely by his extraordinary talent which, in the words of Gunther Schuller, stood "out like a mountain peak over its neighboring foothills."[5]

Cultural heroes make us uneasy nowadays, and the higher the culture, the more skeptical we become. In the area of music, however, this contemporary attitude is more than a result of evolving tastes. Over and above its principal function as a preserver of music, Edison's phonograph had a less noticeable, yet hardly unimportant role in changing society's perception of music and musicians. Following some sort of cultural law of supply and demand, the proliferation of any art form appears to lead inevitably to its devaluation. Just as the photograph has led to a trivialization of the visual image and the spread of printing has lessened the dignity of the written word, so has the easy accessibility of inexpensive recordings led to a devaluation both of the musical performance and the performer.

Those who doubt that any qualitative change has taken place in society's attitudes towards music need only compare the music criticism of one hundred years ago with that produced today. The rapturous praise lavished on the virtuosos of the nineteenth century—Paganini, Liszt, Chopin—has caused many to question whether the great artists of our own time can match those of an earlier age. Yet it is more likely that modern musicians, far from being inferior to their predecessors, have simply suffered from the overexposure which recordings have given to their music. It is hard for us to wax rapturously over a Lazar Berman performance when we can hear it once more, or one hundred times more, at will simply by drawing a record from our shelf and placing it on our turntable. We are no longer inclined, as were music lovers of the past, to attribute diabolical powers to especially adept musicians—as was the case, for instance, with Paganini. In contrast, our age has relegated music to "background music," has replaced listening to music with "having a record on," has pushed music—once the privileged companion of the sacrosanct—out from the churches and concert halls, and into supermarkets, roadside diners, and department stores.

All these forces encourage the contemporary listener to treat music as just one more part of day-to-day life which, thanks to the conveniences of modern society, can be taken for granted. If earlier generations saw music as having a preternatural effect on individuals and felt that the question of music's affective power was as significant in its own way as questions about the origin of the universe and the nature of man, in the twentieth century such issues, to the extent that they are considered at all, are rapidly dismissed as unimportant. Certainly we are far removed from past ages when thinkers used a musical metaphor in speculating about a mysterious "harmony of the spheres," or—like Plato—argued against the use of certain scales because of their overpowering affect on listeners. Rather, we are inclined to view such fastidious concern over the power of music as belonging to naive thinkers of a less sophisticated time and place. Yet as recently as a hundred years ago, leading intellects such as Kierkegaard and Nietzsche were placing comparable emphasis on the emotive qualities of music. One can scarcely attribute such differences in viewpoint to a lack of sophistication; a more persuasive explanation relates this drastic change in attitudes to the mass reproduction and easy availability of music. The progressive attitude of the masses towards art which aesthetician Walter Benjamin saw as being engendered by the mechanical reproduction of these works has simply not taken place: rather than raising the masses up to the level of the work of art, the assembly-line production of culture has lowered the value of the finished product by destroying its uniqueness, by eliminating the special status that has always contributed to art's failure. What we have witnessed has been the reduction of art to the level of the commonplace.

The twentieth century's own distinctive view of music has presented a stark contrast to the effusive idealization of performer and performance which characterized virtually all previous history of discourse on the musical arts. Composer Erik Satie was perhaps the first to grasp the essential difference latent in the modern sensibility: in 1920 he wrote of the advent of "furniture music" which would "fill the same role as light and heat."[6] Satie recognized, in the tastes and attitudes of his time, the incipient yet growing desire for a seamless music, stripped of emotional content as well as the cloying individualism characteristic of the Romanticist past.

The ensuing years have borne out Satie's statement—originally viewed by his audience as an elaborate joke—with striking force, not only in classical music but in the whole range of music expression. In 1924, the same year Louis Armstrong made his New York debut, American radio saw its first singing commercial; a decade later George Owen Squier, a retired general and West Point graduate, pushed music further into the background with his invention of "Muzak"—its etymology coming from a combination of "music" with the more modern-sounding word "Kodak." By the late 1930s, background music was a firmly established part of American culture; and Satie's half-ironic injunction—"Enter no house that does not have furniture music" ["N'entrez pas dans une maison qui n'emploie pas la Musique d'Ameublement"][7] was becoming a simple fact of life.

José Ortega y Gasset, in his 1925 essay on "The Dehumanization of Art," was reaching conclusions similar to those of Satie, although on a much broader plane. For Ortega all twentieth-century art, and not just music, was suffering from the gradual disappearance of the human element. He saw this shift as more than an issue of technology, although he, much like other thinkers who came of age at the turn of the century—Martin Heidegger (born 1889), Walter Benjamin (born 1892), Georg Lukacs (born 1885), and others—saw that technology could have non-scientific aesthetic implications. Yet Ortega believed that this dehumanization largely stemmed from deeper psychological and social motives, eventually rooted in a distaste for the human figure. He summarized this tendency as follows:

When we analyze the new style we find that it contains certain closely connected tendencies, It tends (1) to de-humanize art, (2) to avoid living forms, (3) to see to it that the work of art is nothing but a work of art, (4) to consider art as play and nothing else, (5) to be essentially ironical, (6) to beware of sham and hence to aspire to scrupulous realization, (7) to regard art as a thing of no transcending consequence.[8]

The distaste for living forms was expressed most clearly in the visual arts, with their growing tendency towards abstraction. But for Ortega this was not entirely unrelated to the increasingly ambiguous role of the performer and composer in modern music. "From Beethoven to Wagner," he wrote, "the composer erected great structures of sound in which to accommodate his autobiography."[9] Whereas in the twentieth century "music had to be relieved of private sentiments and purified in an exemplary objectification."[10]

This perspective on music provides a common thread to connect those seemingly disparate approaches to serious music which have flourished over the past several decades. Post-war developments in *musique concrete,* aleatory music and, more recently, in minimalism each presented novel approaches to composition, all equally—if somewhat differently—"dehu-manizing." Even while Ortega was writing, George Antheil was causing a stir with his *Ballet mecanique* (1925), scored for percussion, player pianos and, among other things, air-plane motors. Whether, as in this instance, the composer used the sound of machines, or, as in the minimalism of Steve Reich and Philip Glass, merely employed the monot-ony and repetitiveness which one associates with mechaniza-tion, in any event this was music that reflected a peculiarly modern attitude toward music and the arts. The pervasive influence of minimalism in popular music, as well as the continual growth in all types of background music—in the elevator, in the office, in the dentist's chair, and in almost any other enclosed space—show that this tendency is no aberration on the part of serious composers, but a sign of the radically changed aesthetic sensibility of the twentieth century.

III

At one point in Fellini's film *Orchestra Rehearsal,* rebellious orchestra members overthrow the conductor and replace him with an enormous metronome. Throughout the film, Fellini uses the orchestra as a metaphor for society as a whole and, one suspects, Italian society most of all (one orchestra member's recollection of the "good old days" when the strict discipline of a Toscanini-like conductor kept the orchestra in line, comes across as a not so subtle jab at Italy's fascist past); but the film is equally telling when viewed without any metaphorical interpretation, when seen simply as a commentary on music. The overthrow of the conductor and his replacement with a mechanical device is not an inapt portrayal of the state of the various musical arts in the late twentieth century.

The natural link that once existed between a musical performance and the individual musicians performing it has slowly eroded over the past several decades. A number of events, each of them on the surface innocent enough, have furthered this process: the gradual replacement of live performances with recordings and radio broadcasts; the early move from acoustic to electrical recording technology; the introduction and spread of various electric instruments—guitar, organ, bass—and eventually of synthesizer technology; the increased use of multitracking and overdubbing; the replacement of analog instruments with digital equivalents. Indeed, on a contemporary recording the musician may well be less important than the engineer or software programmer—in fact he may be more of an engineer than a musician in any traditional sense. The result is a strange reversal of roles: whereas early recordings hoped to reproduce the sound of a live performance, today musicians are more inclined to adjust public performances in order to recreate the sound of a studio recording. The last few decades have even witnessed the emergence of a strange, new cultural figure: the performer who no longer performs. Artists as different as Glenn Gould and the Beatles have shown that such a role need be neither obscure nor poorly remunerated.

This confluence of technology and art has added to the "exemplary objectification" of music described by Ortega y Gasset. The extraordinary individualism of nineteenth-century art might have fallen out of favor under any circumstances, but with the gradual mechanization of both musical production and its dissemination, any inertial adherence to a human approach to music was likely to seem old-fashioned and out of place. Non-musical arts were equally affected by the onslaught of technology; in many instances an initial aversion to mechanization was replaced by tacit acceptance or even extreme enthusiasm. Compare, for example, the entry on "Sculpture" in the *Encyclopedia Britannica* of 1911 with its counterpart in the 1960 edition: the 1911 edition suggests that "in the opinion of many artists the use of the mechanical pointing-machine is responsible in a great measure for the loss of life and fire in much of modern sculpture;" in 1960 such misgivings are nowhere expressed—"with the help of a pointing-machine," we are told, "the present mechanical system of carving is easy to learn and free of responsibility because it is mathematically exact."[11]

The prescient English thinker T. E. Hulme, shortly before his premature death in World War I, argued that the "period of exhaustion seems to me to have been reached in romanticism";[12] he anticipated that a new kind of art would come to take its place, one which would be "associated in our minds with the *idea of machinery*."[13] The humanist legacy of the past would be replaced by an antithetical modernism: "You will find a sculptor disliking the pleasing kind of patina that comes in time on old bronze and expressing admiration for the *hard clean surface of a piston rod*."[14] (emphasis mine)

Some of the details of Hulme's predictions were no doubt proven wrong—his claim, for example, that engineers' drawings would come to be considered great works of art has yet to come true—but in his overall vision of twentieth-century culture Hulme was extraordinarily perceptive. Ortega's denunciation, a decade later, of the dehumanization of contemporary art elaborated, with less optimism, on these same themes. For better or worse, the new art was to be purged of the human element, of the overt individualism that had been such a vital element in Western art since the Renaissance.

IV

In this light, Armstrong, and by implication all jazz, must appear as somewhat reactionary. After Armstrong, virtually every aspect of jazz thrusts the human element into the forefront: its emphasis on the individual soloist rather than, as in earlier jazz or in traditional classical music, on the collective sound of the ensemble; its fans' and critics' fascination with—indeed their obsession with—personalities; its continued use of acoustic instruments and its reluctance to embrace many of the technological "advances" outlined above; and perhaps most of all, its defiance of Western music's traditional distinction between composition and performance, in fact, its persistent disdain for any musical division of labor, the jazz musician being both creator and interpreter, soloist and accompanist, artist and entertainer.

As we have seen, this was not always the case in jazz. The earliest recordings of New Orleans jazz reveal a music that left little room for individual soloists, featuring instead a more polyphonic approach in which specific instruments were merged into the sound of the group as a whole. Moreover, the music lacked the pretenses of high art; its practitioners were content to treat their craft as, in Ortega y Gasset's words, "a thing of no transcending consequence." Indeed jazz, at least in its earliest form, fit well with Ortega's description of modern art—collective, casual, often tongue-in-cheek (see, for example, Jelly Roll Morton's frequent use of a whole host of rather embarrassing, at least to modern ears, "novelty" effects—animal imitations, car horns, and the like). But as jazz developed it moved in the opposite direction, increasingly approximating a romanticized nineteenth-century sensibility, with a fixation on musical personalities, a growing preoccupation with individual virtuosity, and, above all, a self-seriousness which bordered on pretentiousness. Jazz, despite its recent origins, was acquiring all of the trappings of premodern art.

The reasons behind this transformation are difficult to pinpoint, yet it is hard to deny that the personal influence of Louis Armstrong was a major, if not the predominant cause of this important change. Armstrong's work in the mid-1920s had an enormous impact in making jazz a soloist's art form; his opening cadenza on "West End Blues," completely unlike anything done before on a jazz recording, was a clarion call signaling the beginning of what amounted to a new art form. Similarly, Armstrong's enormous popularity and world-class stature gave the jazz world its first superstar, and also gave the music a credibility it had never had before. Jazz, for once, was permitted to take itself seriously.

For many listeners this musical revolution was much to be lamented: early New Orleans jazz had offered a pristine and jubilant beauty in which individual expression was tempered by the need to form an ensemble sound—one whose unplanned and extravagant counterpoint was totally unlike anything in the more staid classical tradition. After Armstrong this collective style of jazz became an archaic remnant which could only be found among groups which were intentionally trying to resurrect the sounds of a by-gone era. Although the term "modern jazz" was not to make its appearance for two more decades, these seminal recordings of Armstrong in the 1920s established a tradition which made a later, more overt modernism possible.

V

Louis Armstrong's reputation as an important jazz musician has been undeservedly tarnished by his considerable talents as an entertainer. For the present generation, Armstrong is *not* the innovative trumper of the 1920s but rather the wide-eyed singer of "Hello, Dolly." Armstrong's reputation as an entertainer is certainly well deserved, yet ironically it is his own work that contributed to jazz's demise as an entertainer's art form.

The passing years have enriched our understanding of Armstrong's achievement. His music epitomizes the "sound of surprise" (a felicitous phrase coined by *New Yorker* critic Whitney Balliett) that has come to characterize all great jazz. His extension of jazz's rhythmic vocabulary, his daring innovations in phrasing across bar lines, his pioneering expansion of the trumpet's technical range—all these set a pattern for later evolutions in the music. But with these innovations, Armstrong also paved the way for jazz's destruction as a mass art form. The results of this change were not immediate. The big band era saw jazz firmly entrenched as America's popular music. But this was largely the result of the composer's and arranger's craft in creating hit songs and decidedly not due to the improvisational brilliance of the great musicians of the period. Improvisation has never been the public's cup of tea, and since Armstrong improvisation has slowly come to dominate jazz.

But jazz, like the mythological phoenix, died as popular entertainment only to be reborn as serious art. This rebirth was not achieved without its cost. For what it's worth, the modern jazz artist is permitted to view himself as an artist, yet this new role brings with it certain ambiguities. To what extent can the jazz artist aspire to a larger public? Or, if he renounces mass appeal, how will he be compensated by the various institutions—the conservatories, the foundations, the academies—which legitimize serious music and its practitioners?

These problems are aggravated by jazz's odd relation to the other arts. Jazz's unusual role as a nineteenth-century art in the midst of the twentieth century is Armstrong's lasting legacy to the music which he so profoundly influenced. Yet, in the final analysis, this equivocal legacy may be what attracts us most to this strangely intoxicating music. In a confining and dehumanizing cultural landscape, jazz—with its happy neglect of university degrees, academic journals, and the other trappings of the modern artist—gives us the rare chance to experience art resonant of a far different sensibility. The music's pleasures are perhaps only augmented by its semirespectability, as it takes on the allure of all things not entirely favored by the powers that be. Both in the sphere of popular art and of serious art, jazz remains something of an anomaly: in the midst of a culture craving the "furniture music" of an enclosed, predictable space, it is still willing to brave the elements.

II

Jazz and the
Primitivist Myth

> In what way would the music of savages be inferior to that of civilized man?
>
> HUGUES PANASSIE

I

In his 1969 biography of Louis Armstrong, the French critic Hugues Panassie gave the following evocative account of the trumpeter:

> One feels the intensity with which he lives each moment; one feels his innate goodness, his uprightness, his simplicity. Gifted with an extremely lively sensibility, his reactions are immediate and attractive in their finesse, spontaneity and intuition. He approaches people and things with his entire humanity. . . . If Louis speaks only circumspectly about the music of others—and even his own—it is not through indifference. On the contrary, music is such a natural part of him that he no longer feels the need to talk about it, just as one does not talk about the air one breathes.[1]

Panassie recalled an anecdote which illustrated Armstrong's instinctive approach towards music:

> Music was within him, and a melodic fragment was a voice speaking to him; a tune he caught or the mildest rhythm might rouse echoes in him, thrilling him to the depth of his subconscious. Alix Combelle, the French saxophonist, told me that during one of Louis' visits to Paris they were walking up the rue Pigalle late one night when a horse and carriage went by. The horse's hooves rang out clearly on the pavement and to the accompaniment of this unexpected rhythm, Louis immediately began to sing, to the great astonishment of his companion.[2]

Students of cultural history may recognize in these passages the figure of the "noble savage." Calling attention to the trumpeter's "finesse, spontaneity and intuition," Panassie summons up an image not entirely dissimilar to the following account of the South Sea islanders written by John Hawkesworth in 1773:

> In their motions there is at once vigour and ease; their walk is graceful . . . and their behaviour to strangers and to each other affable and courteous. In their dispositions, also, they seem to be brave, open, and candid, without either suspicion or treachery, cruelty or revenge.[3]

One of the remarkable things about this second account is that its author never visited the South Seas. Hawkesworth was a director of the East India Company, as well as a writer, and had access to the then unpublished journals of Captain James Cook and his fellow passengers Joseph Banks, later to head the Royal Society, and Dr. Solander, a Swedish botanist. He used these documents in concocting a romanticized version of native life which often differed significantly from the first-hand accounts. His sources remained unpublished for over a century, and, consequently, Hawkesworth's inaccuracies were widely disseminated and went largely unchallenged.[4]

Hawkesworth's view of South Sea culture, however, was not without precedent. The figure of the "noble savage" is no modern invention; it has been prominent in French thought at least since the late sixteenth century, and may even have been current in the later days of the Roman Empire. (The historian Priscus describes his encounter with a renegade Greek who, in A.D. 448, was living happily with barbarians north of the Danube and who extolled this existence as being far superior to life among the Romans.) Montaigne's essays *Des Canniballes* and *Des Coches* were among the first modern documents to pursue this line of thought, one which was reflected in later travel literature, such as Hawkesworth's, as well as in the writings of thinkers such as Rousseau and Diderot. These influential intellects saw non-Westernized man as enjoying an innocence and purity—an "innate goodness," to borrow Panassie's phrase—which civilized man, for all his erudition and technological superiority, could not match. This view, however worn with use, gained a certain renewed authority in the early part of the twentieth century with the immense interest generated by primitive art in French intellectual and cultural circles. Works of primitive sculpture began appearing with great frequency in Paris around 1906, and over the next several decades the influence of these works began to be seen first in Europe and later in America in the painting and sculpture of modern artists.

The idealization and theorization of primitivism in French culture was soon followed by an equally enthusiastic—and equally abstract—reception for another import from foreign soil: American jazz. To a certain extent, the two intellectual tendencies fused: the passion for jazz was, in many ways, an extension of the passion for *"les choses Africaines"* which was already a dominant theme in French culture. Such a fusion could be seen, for example, in the work of French composer Darius Milhaud. Milhaud's ballet, *La Creation du Monde,* which premiered in Paris in 1923, showed the composer's strong interest in jazz—an interest evidently spurred by hearing black jazz musicians in Harlem during Milhaud's visit to New York in 1922—while the costumes of the dancers were equally innovative in their use of designs drawn from African sculptures and masks. Milhaud, like other French artists of his generation, was increasingly looking outside of Europe for sources of inspiration. The time-honored traditions of Western culture were felt by many as a terrible burden which stifled rather than enhanced any creative undertaking. In this light, jazz and primitive art were seen as closely allied; both were like a breath of fresh air, full of the vitality and exuberance missing in the more stylized extensions of purely European traditions.

European jazz was only in its infancy when composers such as Milhaud and Ravel began integrating it into their works. Jazz's first passage across the Atlantic probably followed the United States entry into World War I in April 1917. America's sudden reversal of its historical isolation may have stemmed from military motives, but the cultural impact of the Yankee's arrival was by no means insignificant. The U.S. forces included several hundred thousand black soldiers who brought with them their own traditions and distinctive culture. William Haywood, a colonel in one of New York's black regiments, mounted a nationwide search at the time to put together what was, in his words, "the best damn brass band in the United States Army."[5] Backed by a $10,000 donation from businessman Daniel Reid, Haywood scoured the country and even went as far as Puerto Rico in his search for musicians. The resulting ensemble, dubbed the Hellfighters, included bandleader James Reese Europe as conductor and dancer Bill "Bojangles" Robinson as drum major. Although

not conceived as a jazz band, the Hellfighters began including jazz-oriented numbers in their repertoire almost from the
start. The band was also able to break down into smaller
groups for more informal playing sessions, and these probably drew more directly from the jazz traditions back home.
In early 1918 the band covered some two thousand miles in
an extended tour of France, and the group's stunning success
inspired other Army bands to "jazz up" their music. The
350th Artillery Band, under the direction of Lieutenant Tim
Brymm, evolved into what he described as "a military symphony engaged in a battle of jazz." Another ensemble, led by
Lieutenant Will Vodery, was described in the newspapers
as "the jazziest, craziest, best tooting outfit in France."

American jazz did not disappear from Europe with the end
of the war. In 1919 Sidney Bechet, the celebrated New Orleans clarinetist and saxophonist, became the first major jazz
musician to perform in Europe. As part of Will Marion
Cook's Southern Syncopated Orchestra, Bechet played with
great success in France and England, including a command
performance at Buckingham Palace for King George V. Bechet
commented on this event years later in his autobiography
Treat It Gentle: "It was the first time I ever got to recognize
somebody from having seen his picture on my money."[6]

Bechet, born in New Orleans in 1897, grew up in a Creole
environment which flirted with high culture. As a child he
went on occasion to the French Opera, and at home he was
surrounded by a very musical family. He began learning
clarinet at age six, using an instrument borrowed from his
brother, and within a few years began playing with some of
the finest jazz musicians in New Orleans. By the time he
went to Europe with the Southern Syncopators, he had already worked with the likes of King Oliver, Bunk Johnson,
and Freddie Keppard.

Bechet was to make several more trips to France in the

years following the war, finally settling there permanently in
1949. Whereas in America he had often needed to supple-
ment his income by working as a tailor, in France Bechet was
able to live as a respected artist, and died in 1959 a wealthy
man. As Leonard Feather wrote of Bechet in his *Encyclopedia of Jazz*: "In France he transcended jazz fame to become
a national vaudeville figure, an entertainer and personality
in the Maurice Chevalier class."[7] Today a visitor to Paris
can see him commemorated in Rue Bechet, which intersects
Rue Armstrong.

II

Almost from the start, European thinkers of note were inclined to treat this new music as a serious artistic endeavor;
accordingly, much of the best jazz writing from the 1920s and
1930s came not from America but from across the Atlantic.
The Swiss conductor Ernst-Alexandre Ansermet published
an analysis of Bechet's music in 1919 that was amazingly
prescient in its understanding of this new type of music. Ansermet called attention to the improvisational element,
to the rhythmic and tonal characteristics, and to the distinctive role of the blues in early jazz, long before these elements
were well understood in the United States.

Not that Americans were unaware of jazz: as historian
James Lincoln Collier has shown, much was written on jazz
in America during the period that was, after all, the "Jazz
Age."[8] Even so, much of this writing served more to spread
misinformation than to foster an understanding of this new
music. For example, John Tasker Howard's *Our American
Music,* first published in 1931, claimed to cover ragtime,
jazz, and swing music, but displayed little if any understanding of each of these areas.[9] Howard's ignorance of the New
Orleans jazz tradition and his focus on the work of lesser

musicians such as Paul Whiteman, Ted Lewis, and Zez
Confrey was all too typical of early commentaries on jazz.
Yet even after being revised in 1939 and again in 1954, the
book still made no mention of crucial figures such as Scott
Joplin, Duke Ellington, Sidney Bechet, Bessie Smith, or
Fletcher Henderson—all of whom had been performing long
before the first edition of *Our American Music* appeared.
(It is perhaps worth noting, in Howard's defense, that such
demonstrations of misinformation were not restricted to the
1930s. As recently as 1974, the noted composer Virgil
Thompson, in reviewing a book on Charlie Parker for the
New York Review of Books, could pose as an expert on the
subject while incorrectly describing Parker as primarily a
tenor saxophonist! One wonders whether Thompson had ac-
actually read the book he was reviewing or whether he had
even bothered to listen to Parker's major recordings.)

In these early days of jazz studies, many of the most important writers and researchers were European. Three of the
most important of these were Hugues Panassie, Charles
Delaunay, and Robert Goffin. Their pioneering works not
only raised the level of appreciation for jazz in Europe but
began filtering back into the United States in the mid-1930s.
The appearance of Panassie's *Hot Jazz* in America in 1936
remains one of the major turning points in the history of
jazz criticism; the book, despite its flaws, went a long way
towards establishing jazz as a subject worthy of serious study
in its land of origin. Panassie's follow-up book *The Real Jazz*
appeared in 1942 and served to correct the excesses of the
earlier volume while extending its author's influence.

While Panassie and Goffin were working in the areas of
jazz criticism and jazz history, Charles Delaunay was em-
barking on the first of a series of influential discographical
studies. His *Hot Discography* first appeared in France in
1936, and in its many revised editions served for almost two

decades as the standard reference guide to recorded jazz. Delaunay initially eschewed the purely alphabetical approach followed by most later discographers and tried to integrate a historical perspective into his work by classifying styles and attempting to show the music's development. But his task became increasingly difficult with the enormous growth in jazz recording activity after World War II. Jazz's very success soon made all but the most ambitious abandon any attempt at compiling a comprehensive general discography of jazz. The 1948 update of *Hot Discography* was the last complete edition; Delaunay's attempt to publish a multivolume follow-up edition never got beyond the letter H. Dave Carey and Albert McCarthy's *Jazz Directory* was similarly overwhelmed in its efforts: its several volumes, published between 1949 and 1957 stopped at the letter L.

Delaunay, of the three pioneers of jazz studies, had the closest contact with the primitivists in the visual arts. As the son of the celebrated modern painter Robert Delaunay and the artist/designer Sonia Delaunay-Terk, the young Charles was thrust, virtually at birth, into an environment which was, in many ways, the very center of contemporary aesthetic trends. The influence of the primitivists figured prominently in the Delaunay household. Indeed, his parents met through their common interest in African art. Art historian Gustav Vriesen has written about Robert and Sonia:

> They went to the Louvre together often, but not to see the paintings of recent centuries. Rather what attracted them and enriched their talks and their thinking were visits to the Egyptian section, the Assyrian sculpture, the Chaldean art. They were less interested in the stream of history than in the ancient sources of artistic form.[10]

Frequent visitors to the Delaunay household included the poet Guillaume Apollinaire and the sculptor A. P. Archipenko, both closely involved in the primitivist movement. In fact Apollinaire, one of Robert Delaunay's closest friends, moved in with the family for a brief period shortly after Charles's birth in 1911. At the time Apollinaire had been suspected as being involved in the recent theft of the Mona Lisa. Deserted by most of his friends, the poet stayed in Delaunay's studio until the charges were eventually dropped.

Apollinaire was a passionate defender of the artistic merits of African and Oceanic sculpture and is justly viewed today as one of the founders of modern primitivism. The following passage from one of his essays probably reflects the general attitude towards this art of those who frequented the Delaunay household:

> The enthusiasm of today's painters and collectors for the art of fetishes is an enthusiasm for the basic principles of our arts; their taste is renewed through contact with these works. In fact, certain masterpieces of Negro sculpture can compete perfectly well with beautiful works of European sculpture of the greatest periods.[11]

The young Charles Delaunay was thus raised in an environment in which the primitive's unreflecting and instinctive relationship with his art was seen as a positive virtue. The overly refined and self-conscious attitude which the European artist took towards his work was, by comparison, a hindrance, an obstacle to the creative act. Although the savage's supposedly "natural" response to art probably could not be achieved by a twentieth-century European, it stood as an ideal towards which one could aspire. Little wonder that Delaunay along with his contemporaries, would try to make jazz fit the mold of primitive art. Such an association, from their perspective, could only add to the music's allure.

Robert Goffin was also closely associated with the primitivists. A writer of poetry as well as prose, Goffin was an

acknowledged expert on Apollinaire, and the impact of
Apollinaire's thinking is clearly reflected in Goffin's works
on jazz. Indeed Goffin, like so many of jazz's great critics,
was a man whose talents extended far beyond the world of
music. In addition to his career as a writer, he was an authority on rats and eels, and a celebrated criminal lawyer in
Brussels. A native Belgian, Goffin fled the country at the
time of the Nazi invasion, leaving behind a successful practice and a collection of over 3,000 jazz records. The last of
the three to see his works reach the United States, Goffin was
in fact the first to write on jazz. His full-length critical study
Aux Frontieres du Jazz appeared in 1931, and, at a time
when Paul Whiteman was acknowledged as the "King of
Jazz," was both uncompromising and ahead of its time in its
dedication to Louis Armstrong, "the real King of Jazz." With
the appearance of *Jazz: From the Congo to the Metropolitan*
in 1944, Goffin achieved his first American publication. His
book on Louis Armstrong, *Horn of Plenty,* was published in
1947 and was, along with Barry Ulanov's early study of Duke
Ellington, one of the first significant jazz biographies.

These three men—Hugues Panassie, Charles Delaunay,
and Robert Goffin—could well be viewed as the founding
fathers of jazz studies. In criticism, discography, and biography, they made many of the first real steps, at times awkward and uncertain, towards establishing a completely new
area of musical research. Their views, their assumptions, their
biases served as starting points for the next generation of
critics, both in the United States and abroad. For just as
American jazz crossed the Atlantic to take root in Europe,
with jazz criticism Europe returned the favor. By the time
jazz studies began in earnest in the United States, the discipline was already established by these role models from
overseas. As we shall see, jazz still retains to this day the
marks of their initial perspective.

Half a century of jazz scholarship has made it relatively easy to point out in retrospect the flaws in these early forays into jazz studies, yet in comparison with the mixture of misinformation and neglect which preceeded these pioneering works, the achievements of Messrs. Panassie, Goffin, and Delaunay are considerable. Looking back to Goffin's favorable view of Armstrong, Ellington, and Henderson in 1931, one is struck at how closely his critical judgments match today's consensus. These early works are perhaps more dated by their general tone than by any factual or critical discrepancies. Jazz historian Richard Hadlock has referred to this as "the carefully documented gee-whiz attitude." Or as Derek Langridge put it: "If the keyword for the 'twenties is ignorance, that for the 'thirties is enthusiasm." Often limited in their understanding of the musical underpinnings of jazz, these first jazz writers focused instead on the vitality and energy of the "hot" soloist. Jazz, for them, was an intense experience, and a purely musicological approach to it, they felt, would only confuse matters.

Yet even more telling, and somewhat distressing, was their tendency to project this same lack of concern with music theory onto the musicians themselves. They saw the jazz artist as a creature of inspiration who, in his own rough and unskilled way, would forge a musical statement that was of the heart and not necessarily of the mind. As Panassie proclaimed in *The Real Jazz*: "Inspiration without culture can produce beautiful works; culture without inspiration is incapable of doing so."[12] For him, jazz's eminence as an art form depended on its practitioners' lack of sophistication. "In music," he wrote,

> primitive man generally has greater talent than civilized man. An excess of culture atrophies inspiration, and men crammed with culture tend too much to play tricks, to re-

place inspiration by lush technique under which one
finds music stripped of real vitality.[13]

From this perspective, formal training and intellectual rigor
serve only to stifle the jazz musician. The vitality of his art
has no need of these essentially decadent Western practices.

Goffin was perhaps even more extreme than Panassie in his
emphasis on this "enlightened ignorance" of the jazz musician. "Louis Armstrong," he wrote in *Jazz: From the Congo
to the Metropolitan,* "is a full-blooded Negro. He brought
the directness and spontaneity of his race to jazz music."[14]
This stemmed from Armstrong's ability to enter what Goffin
referred to as "the trance." He saw this ability as the crucial
determinant of Armstrong's success. Goffin elaborated on this
talent:

> Besides the two qualities which I have just mentioned—
> imagination and technique—Louis possesses the great gift
> which permits him almost automatically to enter into a
> trance and then to express his sensibility by means of his
> instrument. The other two qualities are possessed to a
> greater or lesser degree by the musicians we have just
> compared to Armstrong. Here is a fact I want you all to
> mull over. Many musicians, particularly among the
> whites, have plenty of natural talent; yet, for these, the
> phenomenon of the trance is rare if not completely non-
> existent. Armstrong's gift is present in a few Negroes—
> Charlie Shavers and Leo Watson, to name but two—but I
> know of no white musician who is able to forget himself,
> to create his own atmosphere, and to whip himself up
> into a state of complete frenzy.[15]

This statement of Goffin's is one of the earliest formulations
of a stereotype which has lingered with jazz until the present
day—a stereotype which views jazz as a music charged with
emotion but largely devoid of intellectual content, and which

sees the jazz musician as the inarticulate and unsophisticated practitioner of an art which he himself scarcely understands.

I would like to call this view the Primitivist Myth. It expresses an attitude, which in one form or another, has colored much of the literature on jazz. When this view is presented as starkly as we find it in Goffin's remarks, the modern reader is likely to feel somewhat uneasy. Musical stereotypes and racial stereotypes seem to get mixed up. Despite the author's intention of praising Armstrong, his comments seem to be clearly, if unintentionally condescending. How else can one interpret his description of the ideal jazz performance as "a state of complete frenzy." Presented in such terms, the jazz performance seems hardly a cultural event and more like a medical affliction, akin to epilepsy or schizophrenia.

Though such an extreme example of this stereotype may seem insulting and patently unjust, a milder form of this same attitude continues to influence many recent discussions of jazz. Performances which fail to attain the frenetic and energetic ideal postulated by this stereotype are usually labeled as "cerebral"—one of the most damning adjectives in jazz's critical vocabulary. In contrast, the most excessive demonstrations of musical chaos are often lavishly praised so long as they are done "with feeling." Note for example, Bill Cole's description of John Coltrane and Elvin Jones from his 1976 biography of Coltrane:

> There are really no words to describe the energy that these two men would exude. After each set they would literally be drenched with perspiration, and I often wondered how they could possibly do this over and over again without catching bad colds or even pneumonia. Just before Pharaoh Sanders entered the band, I remember beginning to watch Trane and wondering how much longer he was going to be able to put out that much

energy. . . . When he played, his intensity was almost
unbearable to watch. He seemed to almost want to en-
velop the instrument, whether that instrument was so-
prano or tenor saxophone. His face always seemed to be
straining to its utmost capacity, and the veins in his face
seemed as if they would pop straight out of his body. He
was truly an awesome figure to watch. And as intense as
Trane could be, Elvin Jones was certainly his equal.
Jones was demonic, constantly whipping and interchang-
ing with Trane during the solos. It wasn't just John
Coltrane and Elvin Jones: they were a pair—and they
both put out an equal amount of energy to the people.[16]

For Cole these are words of highest praise. Their similarity
with Goffin's description of Armstrong's "trance" is striking.

III

Just as critical interest in primitivism and in jazz had first
thrived in the same French intellectual environment, both
found a favorable response in the United States in the mid-
1930s. In 1934, the same year which saw the first major
showing of primitive art in the United States, Panassie
began publishing the periodical *Le Jazz Hot* in both French
and English editions, and that same year *Downbeat* was
launched in the United States—a magazine which even today
remains the preeminent American jazz publication. The next
several years saw the first important books on both jazz and
primitive art published in English. In America as in Europe,
these two areas of artistic achievement seemed destined to go
hand in hand.

Thus even a sophisticated commentator such as Winthrop
Sargeant, whose 1938 book *Jazz, Hot and Hybrid* remains
one of the most perceptive works on the subject, could write
with confidence about jazz:

Those who create it most successfully are the ones who know the least about its abstract structure. The Negro, like all folk musicians, expresses himself intuitively.[17]

Here Sargeant mistakenly assumes that jazz's spontaneity implies a lack of self-awareness on the part of its practitioners. Jazz, from this perspective, is qualitatively different from serious composed music. It springs from inspiration, and not from the intellect. Sargeant's view, as expressed here, is identical with Panassie's claim that jazz is "unconscious of its novelty, [and] untarnished by the slightest design."[18]

The truth of this view is somewhat dubious. Jazz, like all art from an aural/oral tradition, reveals its rigors in ways different from notated/written arts. The absence of a permanent document, whether musical score or printed word, does not indicate that the mental processes involved in the creative act are any less evident in improvised art than in composed art. Improvisation merely changes the time frame of what takes place: it is spontaneous composition. The identity of composer and performer allows this act to take place without the mediation of systems of notation. In fact, such settings call into question Western culture's veneration of the written document, when the creative act itself seems to be more central to our appreciation of art. As jazz pianist Erroll Garner once put it: "No one can hear you read music."

Moreover, the view that jazz was created largely by unschooled and unreflecting musicians who simply "played from the heart" is, at best, highly misleading. As early as Jelly Roll Morton and Pops Foster, if not before, New Orleans musicians were already thinking in fairly theoretical terms about jazz. Morton, like most of the Creole musicians of his day, was familiar with the European tradition in music, and his own compositions and performances show a sense of balance and formal structure which is anything but primitive.

Indeed virtually all of the major piano players of early jazz had some training in the European tradition: Scott Joplin, Tony Jackson, James P. Johnson, Lil Hardin, Earl Hines, Fletcher Henderson, Fats Waller, Count Basie, and Art Tatum—just to name a few—all had formal training on the instrument.

Nor were the other instrumentalists of early jazz entirely unschooled. Coleman Hawkins, the first major tenor saxophonist in jazz, studied music in college, as did a number of later saxophonists including Chu Berry, Willie Smith, and Don Redman. The clarinet, an instrument whose use in jazz stems back even farther than the saxophone, could boast of a number of well-trained early exponents. Alphonse Picou and Lorenzo Tio, both of New Orleans, were quite fluent in the European tradition, and passed down their expertise to many of the younger jazz clarinetists. The Tio household, in particular, served as music school for a list of students that sounds like an honor roll of New Orleans clarinet players, including Johnny Dodds, Barney Bigard, Omar Simeon, Jimmy Noone, and Sidney Bechet. The New Orleans drummer Zutty Singleton could read music—something many contemporary drummers are still unable to do—and worked frequently with the John Robichaux Band in New Orleans. Robichaux, according to Pops Foster, "wouldn't hire anyone who couldn't read."[19]

The European musical tradition figured prominently in the social life of nineteenth-century New Orleans. Grand opera began in the city in 1837, and light opera was performed at least as far back as 1810. The French Opera House, constructed in 1900, held a central place in the city's cultural environment. While the brothels and honky-tonks of Storyville receive most of the attention of jazz scholars, the "serious" music of turn-of-the-century New Orleans played an important and often overlooked role in shaping the first generation of jazz musicians. Both Alphonse Picou and Lorenzo Tio, Sr., for example, played for French opera, and it is clear that many of the arias were familiar to even the non-reading musicians of the time.

In this light it is hard to accept opinions such as those voiced by jazz and ragtime scholar Rudi Blesh:

> With no formal training, the Negroes imparted vocal tone to the cornet, trombone, and even the clarinet, though it is an achieved, not a natural, tone with these instruments. Extreme musicality gave the Negroes quick mastery of even these difficult instruments and helped them to surmount difficulties they did not even know existed. Unable to read music, they promptly transformed the marches into Negro jazz just as their forerunners had transformed the hymn into spirituals.[20]

In point of fact, not all exponents of "Negro jazz" were unable to read or lacked formal training.

This is not to say that all of the practitioners of early jazz had had a thorough training in their instruments. Many of the instruments—notably the cornet and saxophone—were not part of the symphonic tradition, and this limited the practitioners ability to imitate and study under classical players. Some of the best early performers on these instruments were largely self-taught and were, accordingly, poor readers. Moreover, many of the players who had studied formally were still far from achieving conservatory proficiency. Yet in virtually every case this lack of a formal background was not, as with a true primitivist, viewed as an advantage or as a key to inspiration. Many of the prominent musicians of early jazz took great pains to overcome the limitations of their formal training. Johnny Dodds, for example, felt a need for further study even after he had established himself with Kid Ory's band, perhaps the most celebrated New Orleans band of the time. As Pops Foster recalled:

> Johnny Dodds didn't read so good and the only band he had played with was Ory's. When work got tough he was thinking about going to St. Louis or Chicago and wanted to know if I thought he could play with the other bands. I told him he should study and train himself to play with any bands and not just one like he's done. . . . He said, "Yeah George, that's what I did wrong, I got wrapped up around one band and I sound funny with anybody else." After that he studied and could play with all bands.[21]

Armstrong, also a member of Kid Ory's band in the early 1920s, felt a similar need to improve his grasp of fundamentals. In his autobiography *Satchmo,* he wrote:

> Kid Ory's band could catch on to a tune quickly, and once they had it no one could outplay them. But I wanted to do more than fake the music all the time because there is more to music than just playing one style. . . . David Jones played the melophone. He had joined us from a road show that came to New Orleans, a fine musician with a soft mellow tone and a great ability to improvise. I mentioned him particularly because he took the trouble between trips to teach me to read music. I learned very quickly.[22]

Certainly it is hard to agree with Blesh in viewing these musicians' "lack of formal education as a freeing factor in hot and spontaneous creation." These performers succeeded despite their limitations rather than because of them, and their success is a testimony to the inherent vitality in the Afro-American music tradition and not merely the result of musical illiteracy. Yet the primitivist mythology of jazz, borrowed from the first generation of European critics and still echoed by writers today, has fostered a romanticized view of jazz in which the limitations of the music's earliest practitioners have been depicted as their greatest attributes.

IV

Ornette Coleman, of all the major figures of postwar jazz, comes closest to fitting the stereotyped image of the jazz primitive. A pioneer of the *avant-garde* movement, Coleman was often interpreted by well-meaning critics as drawing his innovative approach to jazz from a musical ignorance which served him as a positive asset. As James Lincoln Collier has argued in his excellent historical work *The Making of Jazz*, Coleman "must be seen as a primitive artist."[23] He is quick to add: "I do not mean at all to deprecate him with this term." Coleman's mystique was, if anything, enhanced by this apparent lack of involvement with traditional forms of music, either classical or jazz.

Looking at Ornette on the stage, one could well understand Collier's assessment. Along with his group-mate, trumpeter Don Cherry, Coleman presented a formidable appearance when they first performed in New York in the fall of 1959. Their very instruments invited skepticism: Coleman played a white plastic alto saxophone, an anomaly in the jazz world, while Cherry played a miniature pocket trumpet. Their dress was equally unusual—Ornette had designed distinctive waistcoats for the band. This, combined with their unusual way of playing jazz, was enough to call into question their relation to the jazz tradition. If ever a modernist in jazz could be called a primitive, Ornette would seem to be one.

His background was far from typical for a jazz musician. Coleman was originally from Fort Worth, Texas, where he was born in March 1930. His father died when Ornette was only seven years old, and his mother supported him and a sister through her work as a seamstress. Soon after he entered high school, Ornette began trying to convince his mother to buy him a saxophone. Although the family was hard pressed financially, she eventually met her son's urgent request. "One night she woke me up and told me to look under the bed," Coleman later recalled, "and there was an alto saxophone. I had never touched a horn before."[24]

While still in high school Coleman began working professionally as a musician. His earliest experiences were not, however, in jazz, but in rhythm-and-blues, and his playing acquired a rough gutbucket dimension that was to stay part of Coleman's style well into his "experimental" period. But it did not take long before Coleman was exposed to the music of the bebop players who were then causing such a sensation back East. The tenor saxophonist Red Connors, who occasionally used Ornette with his band, taught him a wide variety of bop compositions which the band would play when circumstances allowed them to depart from their typical rhythm-and-blues repertoire. As Coleman later recalled: "I heard them [Connor's band] play every bebop tune that was recorded between 1943 and 1950. They could play any other composition by any other major guys who were writing bebop music. I knew most of the tunes; I could play those that Bud Powell and Charlie Parker had written and George Shearing had written. Anything that was melodically complicated I thought I had to learn—a bunch of bebop tunes."[25] Coleman's claims of his bebop prowess are probably exaggerated—it's hard to imagine any band mastering "every bebop tune that was recorded between 1943 and 1950." Nonetheless even a more limited exposure to modern jazz would put the lie to the later commentators who argued that Ornette developed *ex nihilo* his approach to jazz.

The early 1950s found Ornette in Los Angeles where work was infrequent and the other musicians often hostile. He would sit in with local jazz bands, and although he knew the standard bebop tunes, Ornette played them differently than the way they had traditionally been played. If his early recordings are any indication of his style at this period, he was probably incurring the wrath of the other performers by using a modal rather than a chordal approach to improvising. In other words he would be working off one or more scales rather than strictly following the chord changes of the song.

Despite frequent rejection from most of the musical establishment, Coleman soon found a few kindred spirits who shared his interest in experimentation. Chief among these was trumpeter Don Cherry, who was to share the limelight with Coleman when both rose to fame a few years later. Other participants in this growing school of jazz dissidents included drummers Ed Blackwell and Billy Higgins, tenor saxophonist James Clay, trumpeter Bobby Bradford, bassist Don Payne, and pianist Walter Norris. In this setting Coleman, although no closer to public acceptance, was able to share his process of musical discovery with other similar-minded individuals, and, in turn, learn from their own attempts at experimentation.

Ornette's first major break came when, through the intervention of bassist Red Mitchell, he was able to meet record producer Les Koenig, who then ran Contemporary Records, a label which specialized in the music of the major West Coast jazz players of the time. Although some of the musicians on the label were involved in experimentation of various sorts, all of the music on the label was quite accessible, clearly tonal in orientation, and definitely more traditional than what Coleman was then doing. Mitchell had suggested that Coleman attempt to sell Koenig his compositions, but felt that a recording of Ornette's performances would probably be out of the question. It was on this basis that Coleman and Cherry approached Koenig.

The audition got off to a bad start. Coleman attempted to demonstrate his compositions on the piano, but having only the most limited ability at the keyboard, he fumbled his way through them and eventually resorted to playing them on the alto with Cherry accompanying on trumpet. Koenig was intrigued enough by what he heard to agree to schedule the pair for a recording session. Soon after, Coleman and Cherry recorded their debut album in a group with Higgins, Norris, and Payne.

Shortly after the release of *Something Else! The Music of Ornette Coleman,* Coleman met John Lewis, pianist and leader of the Modern Jazz Quartet, who took a strong interest in the young altoist. Lewis helped arrange a scholarship for him at the Lenox School of Jazz in Massachusetts, whose faculty that year included composer Gunther Schuller, pianist Bill Evans, drummer Max Roach, and jazz clarinetist/composer Jimmy Giuffre. While at Lenox, Coleman began to attract the attention of a wider group of admirers. On the strength of some favorable notices, Coleman and Cherry were booked into the Five Spot in New York for an engagement that was destined to prove decisive for Ornette and divisive for the jazz world as a whole.

The engagement rapidly became the center of attention in the jazz world, as musicians and critics were forced into one of two camps. One either praised Ornette as the creative leader of new revolutionary and innovative movement in jazz, or one panned him as an inept charlatan who was making more noise than music. Don DeMichael's comments on Coleman's composition "Beauty," which appeared in a *Downbeat* review in May 1961, were typical of the opinions voiced by this second group: "The resulting chaos is an insult to the listening intelligence. It sounds like some horrible joke, and the question here is not whether this is jazz, but whether it is music."[26] Whitney Balliett, writing in the *New Yorker,* was equally skeptical. "At first hearing," he wrote, "he sounds inflexible, crude, and even brutish. His tone appears thick-thumbed and heavy. He plays insane and seemingly purposeless runs."[27]

Coleman's supporters were equally vociferous, and their ranks included some of the most influential names in the music world. Leonard Bernstein declared himself in favor of this new development in jazz, and sat in with Ornette's band one night at the Five Spot. Important jazz critics such as Martin Williams, Nat Hentoff, and John Tynan also were quick to argue in defense of Coleman's music. But on one issue both camps were in agreement: Ornette was a true artistic primitive. He had created his distinctive approach to improvisation in isolation from the jazz tradition rather than as an extension to it. The very title of his debut album—*Something Else!*—immediately claimed for Ornette a position outside of the mainstream. Though he may have been Charlie Parker's spiritual heir—and many claimed just that—he was, from a practical point of view, Parker's antithesis. This was a music that was "outside" rather than "inside" the tonal tradition. Even John Lewis, who tried to relate the music to the bebop tradition of Parker, admitted: "It's not like any ensemble that I've ever heard."[28]

This image of Coleman as a figure from outside of the jazz heritage led to some unusual hypotheses. One commentator speculated that Ornette's style derived from his mistaken use of piano music when learning the saxophone. Deciding that the A in the book was the C on his horn, Coleman supposedly achieved his unique, albeit inadvertent, approach to melodic construction. The anecdote reveals more about the state of jazz criticism than it does Coleman's music. He was, in fact, much more deeply rooted in the jazz tradition than any of his early admirers—or detractors—were willing to admit. The belated release of an informal recording made in 1958 by pianist Paul Bley, featuring both Coleman and Cherry, gives some indication of Ornette's playing before his rapid rise to fame the following year. The altoist's indebtedness to Charlie Parker, both in tone and conception, is evident throughout. A long version of Parker's intricate composition "Klacto-veesedstene" is anything but the work of an unschooled primitive. Little wonder that critic John Tynan, when he heard tapes of the then unknown Coleman's group in 1957, classified the band as a "neo-bop quartet."[29]

Yet even the early recordings Coleman made for the Contemporary and Atlantic labels—viewed by most critics as representing the essence of Ornette's musical revolution—are surprisingly close to the bebop tradition in formal structure and execution. The harmonic structure of the compositions is often drawn from a standard composition such as "I've Got Rhythm" or "Honeysuckle Rose," and the solos often followed a strict thirty-two-bar format. Even Coleman's distinctive melodic approach was hardly as radical a departure from the tradition as it had been made out to be: its basically modal flavor was not dissimilar from what Miles Davis was then doing as part of the jazz "mainstream."

These ties to the jazz tradition were all but overlooked in the period of his first successes. For better or worse, the tag of "primitive" stuck, and in fact probably assisted Coleman in his rise to fame. The idealization of the jazz primitive had long since become a staple of jazz criticism; in his own way, though probably not consciously, Ornette was playing to the critics just as much as Armstrong had been indulging their similar notions a generation earlier. Yet even Coleman soon became wary of the pigeonhole into which he had been thrust. Despite claims to the contrary by writers such as Collier, it is unclear whether the primitive label is ever entirely complimentary to a contemporary artist. The "primitivism" admired by the early critics of African art was representative of an unreflective, organic relationship between art and artist; it was naive in a non-pejorative sense of the word. With Ornette, in contrast, as with other modern artists—for example American primitivist painters such as Grandma Moses—the term is often used seemingly as a euphemism for "ignorant."

In response to this label, Coleman began to surround his music with a whole vocabulary of technical-sounding jargon which resembled, in form if not in content, the theoretical underpinnings of "serious" art. Coleman called this theoretical approach to his music "harmolodics." While the exact nature of harmolodics is by no means easy to convey or even understand—Ornette's writings on the subject being almost impenetrable—the psychological value of having a manifesto, comprehensible or not, was clear: as a theoritician, Coleman could no longer be accused of creating his music in an intellectual vacuum.

Coleman gave a definition of harmolodics in his essay "Prime Time for Harmolodics," which appeared in *Downbeat* in 1983:

> What is harmolodics? Harmolodics is the use of the physical and mental of one's own logic made into an expression of sound to bring about the musical sensation of unison executed by a single person or with a group. Harmony, melody, speed, rhythm, time, and phrases all have equal position in the results that come from the placing and spacing of ideas. This is the motive and action of harmolodics.[30]

In recent years, Coleman's theorizing bent has been almost as influential as his music was in the late 1950s and early 1960s. The "science" of harmolodics has found a number of dedicated disciples, especially among the many musicians Coleman has played with. Guitarist Blood Ulmer told interviewer Chip Stern: "With harmolodic music I hope to find a balance between the body and the mind."[31] Bassist Jamaal-adeen Tacuma was equally enthusiastic, if no less vague. "Through playing harmolodically," he remarked, "I've developed the ability to make my patterns move in sequential order when I'm improvising . . . what I try to get going is a succession of notes that move in a compositional direction." One can only echo critic Gary Giddins's response to this cryptic formula. "One wonders," he writes, "in what direction they think the notes of Jimmy Blanton or Lester Young or practically every great improviser in jazz history are moving if not in a compositional one."

Despite the ambiguities of these abstract formulations of their craft, such statements serve at least one genuine need on the musicians' part. They are a clear declaration that the artists themselves view what they are doing as a serious enterprise requiring the mastery of a difficult body of knowledge. Ornette Coleman, more than most, knows the bitterness of comments such as "he's just fakin' it" or "he can't play the horn." Although the romanticist notion of the inspired primitive—one who creates beauty out of pure ignorance—may have some appeal to the jazz critic or writer, to the jazz musician it's just one more way of keeping his work separate from the "serious" traditions of Western culture. In this sense, manifestoes such as Coleman's statement on harmolodics possess a certain truth of their own—a truth, however, which even Coleman's most fervent admirers may have overlooked.

V

Only a century ago, John Ruskin could proclaim with a clear conscience that there was "no art in the whole of Africa, Asia or America." The Victorian sensibility was not embarrassed by such Eurocentric opinions: it was an age which often equated artistic merit with refinement and technical mastery, and which could still perceive Western art as following a path of progress almost as surely and inevitably as were the natural sciences.

The ensuing decades saw a striking reversal of this attitude. Today the notion of progress in the art world seems almost ludicrious—although it still exerts its influence in hidden ways—and the proud and defiant faith in the European tradition, epitomized by Ruskin's comment, has clearly been shaken if not yet toppled. The positivism of the nineteenth century has given way to, at best, a half-hearted relativism, or, at worst, an expressed dislike for all things smacking of civilization. Art criticism has been only one of the disciplines affected by this pronounced reversal of values; virtually all of the social sciences have also, to some extent, grown equally suspicious of the once unchallenged advantages of Western life. Because of this radical shift in values, many may well be comforted by a view of jazz which links it with the non-European traditions of primitive art. The music's undeniable vitality seems somehow more assured and impressive if its ties to Western culture are severed. Such a view, however incorrect or misleading it might be, brings with it some solace.

In point of fact, jazz is not primitive art. Nor, like the works of Picasso or Modigliani, is it imitative of primitive art. The jazz artist could not achieve the naive attitude of the Lascoux cave painter even if he tried. And far from trying to imitate such artlessness, the jazz musician has strived, from as far back as we can trace, to increase his level of sophistication and his knowledge of his craft. Indeed jazz music, more than most modern art forms, retains an adherence to old-fashioned standards of technical proficiency; the belief that an artist need merely be inspired to produce great art, that technique is no substitute for creativity and may even detract from it—this attitude may have found advocates in some schools of modern poetry or modern painting, but has made little headway in the world of jazz. Even members of jazz's *avant-garde* are expected, by both critics and colleagues, to be fluent in the technically demanding bebop repertoire. The idealization of an instinctive and intuitive approach to musical performance, implicit in the primitivist view of jazz, bears little if any resemblance to that music as it is actually played.

Certainly jazz is not the only art which suffers from this confused notion of primitivism. A few years ago, the Museum of Modern Art in New York devoted an exhibition to "Primitivism in Twentieth-Century Art" in which works by artists such as Paul Klee and Alberto Giacometti were shown side by side with primitive artifacts. The curators of the show seemed to feel that the extraordinary gulf which separated such different works was more than compensated for by their similar appearance. Art critic Arthur Danto, writing in *The Nation,* was one of the few to object to the strange assumptions underlying these pairings:

> One watches the visitors playing the imposed game of resemblances, pointing with excitement to the meaningless similarities the framers of the exhibition have assembled for their edification. It is an unhappy experience to observe these hopeful pilgrims coerced by as acute an example of museological manipulation as I can think of. The only outcome can be a confusion as deep as that which underlies the entire array.[32]

Danto, in addition to being an art critic, is a respected academic philosopher, and his training in analytic thought makes him, no doubt, more sensitive than most museum-goers to such discrepancies. But one should not need a graduate degree in philosophy to see the confusion inherent in such romanticized images of primitive art. Even the leap of faith involved in calling such works "art" is open to criticism—their role in primitive culture is something we may never fully understand—but the pairing of such artifacts with works of modern art clearly does a gross injustice to both groups of objects.

Such curatorial excesses notwithstanding, jazz has suffered even more than the visual arts from half-baked ideas about primitivism. Yet if the Primitivist Myth were merely a misguided interpretation of jazz history, its excesses, although regrettable, would not be a source of major concern. The problem lies in the fact that this mythology of jazz has extended its influence far beyond the area of historical research. It has come to shape the critical standards which define the art form, and its impact is all the more damaging, given that its influence is rarely stated openly. Rather, like some unmentioned *a priori* line of reasoning, it colors critical judgments while rarely submitting itself to critical scrutiny.

One result of this is a false opposition, posed repeatedly in the literature of jazz, between music of inspired creativity, on the one hand, and that of "cold" intellectualism, on the other. The implication here is that jazz musicians can or should aspire to states of inspiration that "transcend" or "stop short of" mental processes. But such an opposition can hardly be said to exist. Anyone who has performed jazz can attest to the immense powers of concentration required in the moment of improvisation; the state of apparent distraction described by so many writers on jazz—what Goffin called the "trance"— is by no means an attitude of forgetfulness but is rather a sign of the musician's intense involvement with the performance. Such concentration on the music is not an indication of any lack of ability on the performer's part. It is, in fact, quite essential: the necessity that jazz be *improvised*—the requirement of spontaneity—increases rather than decreases the demands on the artist. Put simply, the creation of jazz requires more than mere visceral energy.

Further, such a glorification of primitivism encourages many of the worst aspects of jazz culture. It creates a general impression among musicians, both established and aspiring, that discipline is not required in learning or performing jazz; that a firm technical mastery of one's instrument is either unnecessary or positively to be avoided as stifling the creative impulse; that emotional immediacy is to be preferred over clarity and sophistication; and finally, that the various well-publicized excesses of the jazz musician's personal life are not problems to be avoided but signs that the musician has achieved a special intensity of existence that sets him apart from his peers. Indeed excesses of all kinds are apparently to be encouraged. Restraint, discipline, reflection, self-criticism—while these may be adequate virtues for artists practicing in the decadent Western tradition, such qualities have little to do with primitive art and, by implication, with jazz.

True, one can hope that the great artist will impose discipline upon himself—that even outside the confines of a conservatory or university, the exceptional talent will fill in the gaps in his playing and undertake the labors that are necessary to insure mastery of his craft. In point of fact, jazz history does provide examples of exactly this type of striving for perfection. Yet at the same time, the jazz world displays an even greater abundance of mediocrity, indifference, empty posturing, and empty music.

Certainly the question must be raised whether the Primitivist Myth has served jazz well. Perhaps at some earlier stage in the music's development, it played an important part in romanticizing and popularizing an art form that was hindered more by neglect than by critical excesses. But in the cold light of the present day, such a mythology of jazz appears to have long outlived its questionable usefulness. Now, uncritically assumed in so much thinking and writing on jazz, it threatens to become a self-fulfilling prophecy, creating a music which fits its unrelenting stereotype of an intellectually void and unreflecting art form.

III

The Imperfect Art

Jelly Roll Morton, the celebrated New Orleans pianist and composer, often asserted that he had invented jazz in 1902. Morton, as even his admirers admit, was a man prone to exaggeration, particularly on the subject of his own achievements. Yet even if we had no other reason to doubt him, this extraordinary claim would probably still make us uneasy. How could anyone *invent* jazz? It seems rather to be like electricity or North America—things not consciously invented, but only recognized, after the fact as it were, by some especially observant or fortunate individual.

Those with a taste for historical exactitude may feel comforted by imagining some definite date in the past when musicians, perhaps on cue from Jelly Roll or one of his contemporaries, threw away their written scores and started to improvise. The history of jazz, however, is scarcely so tidy; even the earliest Afro-American musicians were apparently playing without written parts, and improvisation, far from starting with jazz, has a rich history as old as music itself.

Yet improvisation, if not restricted to jazz, is nonetheless essential to it. Morton's music, as well as that of other early jazz masters—Louis Armstrong, King Oliver, Sidney Bechet, and their contemporaries—reflects its central role. More than any of these artists' compositional or technical innovations, improvisation remains even today the most distinctive element of a jazz performance—so much so that a jazz instrumentalist is evaluated almost entirely on his ability as a soloist. Certain composed works—Gershwin's *Rhapsody in Blue,* for example—may sound "jazzy," but what we hear is not jazz until the spontaneous element of improvisation is added to the written parts.

For the trained musician, this calculated disregard of the written score can prove to be exasperating. Pianist Lillian Hardin, later to become Mrs. Louis Armstrong, studied music for three years at Fisk University before becoming involved with jazz. Such formal training was of little use, however, when she auditioned for her first job in a jazz band. Hardin later recalled:

> When I sat down to play I asked for the music and were they surprised! They politely told me they didn't have any music and furthermore never used any. I then asked what key would the first number be in. I must have been speaking another language because the leader said, 'When you hear two knocks, just start playing.' It all seemed very strange to me, but I got all set, and when I heard those two knocks I hit the piano so loud and hard they all turned around to look at me. It took only a second for me to feel what they were playing and I was off.[1]

If improvisation is the essential element in jazz, it may also be the most problematic. Perhaps the only way of appreciating its peculiarity is by imagining what twentieth-century art would be like if other art forms placed an equal emphasis on improvisation. Imagine T. S. Eliot giving nightly poetry readings at which, rather than reciting set pieces, he was expected to create impromptu poems—different ones each night, sometimes recited at a fast clip; imagine giving Hitchcock or Fellini a handheld motion picture camera and asking them to film something, anything—at that very moment, without the benefits of script, crew, editing, or scoring; imagine Matisse or Dali giving nightly exhibitions of their skills—exhibitions at which paying audiences would watch them fill up canvas after canvas with paint, often with only two or three minutes devoted to each "masterpiece."

These examples strike us as odd, perhaps even ridiculous, yet conditions such as these are precisely those under which the jazz musician operates night after night, year after year. Jazz demands that the artist create something new and different at every performance; musicians who "cheat" by playing the same or similar solos over and over again are looked down upon by colleagues and fans. In 1978, David Hollenberg wrote in criticism of a performance by pianist Ray Bryant:

> How much is improvised? Tonight, Bryant played *After Hours* in a note-for-note copy of the way he played it on the *Dizzy, Rollins, and Stitt* album on Verve some fifteen years ago. Was it written then? Or worse. Has he transcribed and memorized his own solo, as if it were an archeological classic? It was fine blues piano indeed, but it is odd to hear it petrified in this way. Similarly, Bryant concluded each set tonight with a gospelish blues (in C, of course) that was, note-for-note, the same both times. The hall had been cleared at the break, so the few of us that snuck through both sets were faced with the strange

fact that some of the freest sounding pieces of the evening were the most mechanical.[2]

Here it is not the musical quality of Bryant's performance
that is under attack—Hollenberg admits that the piece in
question was "fine blues piano indeed"; instead, it is the lack
of the crucial improvisational element which disturbs the
critic.

Bryant's case is not unusual. Most jazz musicians find it
far easier to rely on certain stock phrases which have proven
themselves effective in past performances than to push themselves to create fresh improvisations. Albert Lord, in his land-
mark work *The Singer of Tales,* has shown that this practice
is also common to the oral poetry tradition and probably
reaches back to Homer, if not earlier.[3] The daunting task of
improvisation, whether in music or poetry, can scarcely be
achieved without some reliance on these memorized phrases.
Even so, Hollenberg's criticism is justified: any style that is
based entirely on these clichés rarely sustains our interest. For
the jazz musician this conflict between his need for spontaneity and his equally strong desire to stay within the confines of the familiar lies at the heart of his music. This is an
aesthetic choice he cannot avoid. And though some have
suggested that jazz is an intuitive art which defies conscious
reflection and, hence, has little to do with aesthetic decisions,
in this instance I would argue that they are wrong. Jazz is as
much an intellectual as an emotional art.

II

Yet does not jazz, by its reliance on spur-of-the-moment improvisation, relegate itself to being a second-rate, imperfect
art form? Does not its almost total lack of structure make even
the best jazz inferior to mediocre composed music? Why, we
ask, should the spontaneous prattle of an improvising musi-

cian interest us as much as the meticulously crafted master-pieces of the great composers? The dilemma jazz faces was stated with clarity by composer Elliott Carter, when he suggested that the musical score serves the essential role of preventing "the performer from playing what he already knows and leads him to explore other new ideas and techniques."[4]

One is tempted to reply that some of the most gifted composers of Western music—Beethoven, Bach, Mozart—were themselves skilled improvisers who took great interest in the challenge of spontaneous creation. But this is more of an evasion than an answer. That Mozart improvised in his spare time is no more a reason for glorifying improvisation than is the fact that Mozart enjoyed bawdy jokes a reason for elevating them into an art form. Our problem remains, and despite its neglect by most jazz critics, it is the central problem of jazz criticism. It has become a commonplace to assert that jazz is an "art"; yet those who glibly pronounce this word seldom move on to a discussion of how jazz compares (if at all) with the established arts. If jazz music is to be accepted and studied with any degree of sophistication, we must develop an aesthetic that can cope both with that music's flaws as well as its virtues.

It is hardly worth noting that the improvisations of Beethoven could scarcely have been as perfect as his compositions; still I feel confident that I am not alone in being willing to exchange—were such an exchange possible—half a dozen of his written works for just one recording of Beethoven improvising at the keyboard. Can I justify this desire on the grounds of something more than idle curiosity? Must improvised art be branded as second-rate art—as art which is necessarily less worthy of our attention than that which is the result of careful planning? If we hope to elaborate a conceptual framework which will allow us to accept jazz on its own terms—and not as the bastard child of composed music—we must develop what I would like to call an "aesthetics of imperfection."

An aesthetics of jazz would almost be a type of non-aesthestics. Aesthetics, in principle if not in practice, focuses our attention on those attributes of a work of art which reveal the craftsmanship and careful planning of the artist. Thus the terminology of aesthetic philosophy—words such as form, symmetry, balance—emphasizes the methodical element in artistic creation. But the improviser is anything but methodical; hence these terms have only the most tangential applicability to the area of jazz. The very nature of jazz demands spontaneity; were the jazz artist to approach his music in a methodical and calculated manner, he would cease to be an improviser and become a composer. For this reason the virtues we search for in other art forms—premeditated design, balance between form and content, an overall symmetry—are largely absent in jazz. In his act of impulsive creation, the improvising musician must shape each phrase separately while retaining only a vague notion of the overall pattern he is forging. Like the great chess players who, we are told, must be able to plan their attack some dozens of moves ahead, the jazz musician must constantly struggle with his opaque medium if he hopes to create a coherent musical statement. His is an art markedly unsuited for the patient and reflective.

III

Perhaps this unremitting emphasis on spontaneity helps to explain the peculiar personalities of so many of jazz's most noted practitioners. If the jazz artist is impatient and unpredictable, it is only because his art stresses precisely those mercurial qualities. This is not to say that the jazz life breeds unreliability or instability. The line of causation probably moves in the opposite direction: the jazz world offers a creative outlet for the musical talents who, for often unrelated reasons, lack the patience and decorum to succeed in the more traditional areas of musical activity. One can scarcely imagine a Charlie Parker or a Lester Young thriving in an environment which demanded the production of elaborate symphonic scores, or the ability to survive in the academic milieu of the conservatory or university music department. For artists such as these, jazz provides the most suitable area in which they can develop and exercise their talents. Indeed, only a particular type of temperament would be attracted to an art form which values spur-of-the-moment decisions over carefully considered choices, which prefers the haphazard to the premeditated, which views unpredictability as a virtue and sees cool-headed calculation as a vice. If Mingus, Monk, Young, and Parker had been predictable and dependable individuals, it seems unlikely that their music could have remained as spontaneously unpredictable or as innovative.

Even the most dispassionate admirer of jazz must find it unsettling to dwell upon the recurring historical correlation between improvisational brilliance and mental instability among jazz's foremost musicians. This disturbing tradition, as old as jazz itself, stretches back to the enigmatic turn-of-the-century figure Buddy Bolden—by most accounts the first musician to play New Orleans style jazz—whose performing career was cut short in 1906 by his lapse into paranoid schizophrenia. For another quarter of a century Bolden survived in a mental institution, finally succumbing to cerebral arterial sclerosis in November 1931; but his music was scarcely so long-lived: no recording of his playing has ever surfaced (although rumors of a pre-1900 cylinder recording have circulated for years), and what we know about it comes only from intriguing and often contradictory descriptions by those who had heard Bolden play. About the only detail these accounts agree on is the loudness of Bolden's playing. The classic account is Morton's, which describes how Bolden's horn could be heard ten or twelve miles away on a clear, still night.[5] In the words of Frankie Dusen: "Bolden blew the loudest horn in the world."[6] Another old-time jazzman remarked on another aspect of Bolden's playing which is perhaps more to the point, at least in its emphasis on the acute psychological pressure which an improvising musician can bring to bear on himself in attempting to remain innovative and creative: "That fellow studied too hard," he said of Bolden, "always trying to think up something to bring out. He could hear you play something and keep it in his head—then go home and think up parts."[7] Morton's evocative characterization of Bolden's disorder is hardly so elegant: "he went crazy because he really blew his brains out through the trumpet."[8] Bolden's recurring appearance in jazz lore as an almost legendary founding figure serves as an apt, if somewhat distressing, reminder of how often jazz's foremost practitioners have lingered at the far end of eccentricity and on the borderline of mental disorder.

In any event few can deny that, as jazz developed, its leading innovators began using their music to display a frenzied, devil-may-care attitude which stressed the most demanding elements in the improvisational process. At the same time this more progressive approach to the music was well suited to the technical virtuosity which many postwar jazz artists brought to their craft. The founders of modern jazz—Dizzy Gillespie, Charlie Parker, Bud Powell—favored breakneck tempos, far faster than those of even the most spirited numbers of the big band era. Whatever time the early jazz musician had to contemplate his solo leisurely as he played it was soon forsaken as modern jazz developed. Parker and Gillespie attacked the chord progressions of songs such as "Cherokee" and "I've Got Rhythm" at such furious tempos that the soloist often had only a mere second to adjust to a chord before the next one was upon him. Hitherto jazz had relied upon the spontaneous creativity of its musicians, but now it seemed that it was their reflexes that were being tested. To the old-timers of jazz, these frantic and frenetic performances could be quite unnerving. Even an intelligent and adventurous swing era musician such as drummer Dave Tough found his first experience with modern jazz to be a frightening one. Tough recalled:

> As we walked in, see, these cats snatched up their horns and blew crazy stuff. One would stop all of a sudden and another would start for no reason at all. We could never tell when a solo was supposed to begin or end. Then they all quit at once and walked off the stand. It scared us.[9]

The heirs of the beboppers valued these same attributes: speed, virtuosity, intensity, and stamina. With the recording of John Coltrane's extraordinarily difficult composition "Giant Steps" in 1959, the development of these musical obstacle courses reached a level of complexity that was almost perverse in the demands it made on the soloist.

With the coming of the new wave of *avant-garde* jazz musicians, the improvisational element in jazz was further emphasized in a different manner. Earlier generations of jazz musicians had incorporated improvised solos into a framework of music that was still largely composed. If we study the earliest jazz recordings, we notice that only a small portion of the music was devoted to improvised solos; even in early modern jazz a great number of compositional elements remained—with the beboppers at least the harmonic progressions and some melodic lead lines were set in advance. But with the assault of the *avant-garde,* even these last vestiges of composed music were often discarded. This reliance on total improvisation had been attempted earlier, for example, by pianist Lennie Tristano and other progressive musicians of the cool school, but these tentative forays into the unknown were only child's play when compared with the more iconoclastic works of the next generation of innovators. (Perhaps it is misleading to speak of "generations" in the context of jazz where important innovations are separated by only a few years. Harmonic developments that occurred over centuries in classical music took hold in the jazz world over a few decades; the development of jazz harmony between 1940 and 1960 is in many ways equivalent to the developments in Western harmony between 1780 and 1920.) By the early 1970s total improvisation had spread from the *avant-garde* back into mainstream jazz. Keith Jarrett's *Solo Concerts,* released during this period, contains two hours of highly melodic and easily accessible music, not a single note of which was composed in advance; Jarrett claims to enter his solo concerts with no preconceived notions of what he is to play, and his confident reliance on the inspiration of the moment is at times almost frightening.

Perhaps the most salient tendency in the history of jazz is the music's increasing reliance on the improvisational element. Even with the earliest practitioners this aspect was present, but, as jazz matured, improvisation came to play a greater and greater role, at first accounting for only a small part of the music, now often accounting for almost all of it. As though it were following some musical law of entropy, jazz has evolved away from the firm ground of composed music towards the *terra incognita* of complete improvisation.

If improvisation is, as I have claimed, the problematic element in jazz, it has only become more so with the passing of time. Some see this increasing reliance on improvisation as a step towards total artistic freedom. Others, less sanguine, see the music falling into the abyss of formlessness.

IV

Certainly it is wrong to claim that there is *no* form in improvisational music; it is rather a different type of form. We must distinguish between two different ways of adhering to form if we are to understand how jazz differs from most of the other arts. I would like to call these two different types of form the blueprint method and the retrospective method.

The blueprint method is most clearly represented, as one might gather from its name, in architecture. Here the artist plans in advance every detail of the work of art before beginning any part of its execution. For the architect this plan takes the form of a blueprint; for the painter it is revealed in preliminary sketches; for the novelist it is contained in outlines and rough drafts.

Some may feel that the blueprint method is the only method by which an artist can adhere to form. From this point of view form is, almost by definition, that aspect of art which adheres to a pre-existing plan—in other words, without some sort of a blueprint, there can be no form. Nonetheless, one can imagine an opposite approach to art: the artist can start his work with an almost random maneuver—a brush stroke on a canvas, an opening line, a musical motif—and then adapt his later moves to this initial gambit. A jazz improviser, for example, might begin his solo with a descending five-note phrase and then see, as he proceeds, that he can use this same five-note phrase in other contexts in the course of his improvisation.

This is, in fact, what happens in Charlie Parker's much analyzed improvisation on Gershwin's "Embraceable You." Parker begins with a five-note phrase (melodically similar to the "you must remember this" phrase in the song "As Time Goes By") which he employs in a variety of ingenious contexts throughout the course of his improvisation. Parker obviously created this solo on the spot (only a few minutes later he recorded a second take with a completely different solo, almost as brilliant as the first), yet this should not lead us to make the foolish claim that his improvisation is formless.

Improvisation follows not the blueprint method but this second approach. The improviser may be unable to look ahead at what he is going to play, but he can look behind at what he has just played; thus each new musical phrase can be shaped with relation to what has gone before. He creates his form *retrospectively*. The same technique can be applied to other arts, but this is generally the exception rather than the rule. A noteworthy example would be Jack Kerouac's novel *On the Road*, which was reputedly typed on a roll of paper instead of on individual sheets; thus the novel was written in a continuous manner without the benefit of rewrites. (It is perhaps worth noting that Kerouac was one of Charlie Parker's greatest admirers, and was known to remark that he would like his writings viewed as a kind of literary counterpart to a jazz improvisation.) Kerouac's novel is a rare exception, if only because most artists want to take advantage of any benefits that may accrue from careful planning or rewriting. Such works are also likely to meet with resistance from audiences, as well as critics, who believe that great art requires more than mere spontaneity. Truman Capote best articulated this view in his acerbic critique of Kerouac's book: "It is not writing," asserted Capote, "it is only typing."

Typically the retrospective method will be employed either by the artist who is extremely impatient, or else by the artist who is under acute time pressure. One of the clearest examples of this institutionalized haste is found in early Italian fresco painting. The *gesso* on which the fresco was painted dried very quickly, so the artist was obliged to complete that portion of the painting with great speed. Bill Evans, in his liner notes to Miles Davis's *Kind of Blue*, describes a similar approach found in a school of Japanese art:

> . . . the artist is forced to be spontaneous. He must paint on a thin stretched parchment with a special brush

and black water paint in such a way that an unnatural or
interrupted stroke will destroy the line or break through
the parchment. Erasures or changes are impossible. These
artists must practice a particular discipline, that of allow-
ing the idea to express itself in communication with their
hands in such a direct way that deliberation cannot
interfere.[10]

The notion that deliberation interferes with the artistic process fits well with the spontaneous demands of improvisation,
yet it is at odds with the much different attitude found in arts
built upon the blueprint method. Examples from the visual
arts notwithstanding, jazz is the most extreme example of a
reliance on retrospective form. Although other performance
arts (theater, choreography) have experimented with improvisation, such attempts have usually been peripheral to
the art form as a whole; certainly none have allowed improvisation to play as dominant a role as has become the case with
jazz. The reasons for this are all the more interesting when
one discovers that they are completely external to the art
forms themselves.

V

Who has exerted the greatest influence on twentieth-century
art? Joyce? Pound? Eliot? Picasso? Le Corbusier? Most would
dismiss such a question as being alluring yet fruitless. The
artistic pantheon is the truest exemplar of pluralism—works
of art are incommensurable, particularly when the works in
question are taken from different artistic realms. How can
we assert that Picasso's *Guernica* is more important than
Proust's *Remembrance of Things Past* when we are unsure
of the very grounds on which such comparisons should be
made? For this reason, the conventional logic goes, it is best

to leave such ratings to those who evaluate prizefighters or hit records.

But even with this acknowledged, I still believe that there was one person whose influence on twentieth-century art surpassed the rest, and this is all the more peculiar when we consider that he himself was not primarily an artist. The extraordinary individual I am referring to is Thomas Alva Edison. The influence of this autodidact inventor from Milan, Ohio, is probably overlooked for the simple reason that it is so pervasive; his inventions set off repercussions in ways that Edison himself would never have understood. His invention of the motion-picture camera was his clearest contribution to the arts; not only did this development make the cinema possible, but Edison's own early forays into filmmaking were among the most significant demonstrations of the potential of this art form.

But there is at least one more art form indebted to Edison— jazz. In 1877 Edison was the first to apply already existing technology in inventing the phonograph; now for the first time sounds could be recorded with the same precision that books achieved in recording words. Few realize how important the existence of the phonograph was to the development of improvised music. Hitherto, the only method of preserving musical ideas was through notation, and here the cumbersome task of writing down parts made any significant preservation of improvisations unfeasible. But with the development of the phonograph, improvised music could take root and develop; improvising musicians who lived thousands of miles apart could keep track of each other's development, and even influence each other without ever having met.

Perhaps we can now answer the question posed above. Why, we asked, has improvised music reached a level of sophistication not found in, for example, improvised theater or improvised dance? The reason is fairly clear: the development of the phonograph made it possible for musical improvisers throughout the world to share a common heritage and react to the innovations of others. The more recent introduction of low-cost video recorders may well allow improvisational theater or dance to follow a similar path.

This is not to make the absurd claim that jazz did not exist before it was recorded; in fact jazz had been developing in New Orleans for some two decades before the historic recording session of February 26, 1917, at which the Original Dixieland Jass Band (ironically a group containing only white musicians) made the first jazz record. Yet the existence of the recording industry was necessary if jazz were to develop at all, rather than die out as a passing fad or persist as mere folk music. The clarinet player Buster Bailey claimed that the musicians in Memphis began to improvise only after they had heard recordings made by the New Orleans players. As the jazz scholar James Lincoln Collier has noted, before jazz was preserved on records it "was an obscure folk music played mainly by a few hundred blacks and a handful of whites in New Orleans, and rarely elsewhere."[11]

These early recordings found a ready audience, and other bands sprang up to fill the public's growing demand for jazz. Only two years after these first recordings were made, Leon "Bix" Beiderbecke, who was destined to be one of the legendary figures of early jazz, developed his own style by studying them. His biographer describes how Bix would place the wind-up gramophone to the left of the family piano and pick out the lead instrument's melody note for note. To catch the more complex phrases he would slow down the gramophone manually. Only through this laborious imitation of recorded jazz was Beiderbecke able to develop his own celebrated style.[12]

This reliance on recordings was repeated again and again

by most of jazz's greatest innovators. It is no exaggeration to suggest that phonograph records were often the early jazz musician's substitute for a conservatory education. They were frequently his only means of assimilating the tradition—how else could Bix Beiderbecke, isolated in Davenport, Iowa, have developed as a jazz instrumentalist? Yet even more striking is the case of Henry "Red" Allen, Jr.: Allen, one of Louis Armstrong's most talented followers, studied the master's music through phonograph records even though he, unlike Beiderbecke, was living in New Orleans contemporaneously with Armstrong! Charlie Parker, perhaps the most original stylist in the history of jazz, similarly served his apprenticeship at the gramophone. Most jazz scholars agree that the turning point in Parker's musical development occurred when he began studying and memorizing the recorded improvisations of tenor saxophonist Lester Young; just as years before Young had benefited from studying the recordings of Frankie Trumbauer. This line of influence continues unabated today: the number of instrumentalists who have been enriched by studying Parker's own recordings is legion—it would include virtually every noteworthy jazz saxophonist since the end of World War II. Time and time again it has been the recording, rather than the live performance, that has propelled the development of jazz over its brief but rich history.

By the time Thomas Edison died in 1931, jazz had swept the nation; the second generation of jazz musicians—Duke Ellington, Coleman Hawkins, Lester Young—had already begun performing. President Hoover, wishing to mark Edison's passing with an elaborate ceremonial gesture, suggested that the great dynamos that provided America with power should be stopped for three minutes in honor of the man who had contributed so much to American technology. Hoover's advisers rejected the plan; the consequences of shutting America down, even for only a few minutes, would be catastrophic. Edison, it seems, had helped to unleash powers which no one could stop, and the implications Edison himself had only vaguely grasped. In the world of art as well, Edison's pioneering inventions unleashed forces which are still reverberating in those two great art forms—the cinema and jazz—which were born in the twentieth century.

VI

After having seen how peculiar jazz is in comparison with other arts, we may despair of justifying it as a true art form rather than as an elaborate craft. Improvisation is doomed, it seems, to offer a pale imitation of the perfection attained by composed music. Errors will creep in, not only in form but also in execution; the improviser, if he sincerely attempts to be creative, will push himself into areas of expression which his technique may be unable to handle. Too often the finished product will show moments of rare beauty intermixed with technical mistakes and aimless passages. Why then are we interested in this haphazard art? What we are talking about is, as I have stressed, an aesthetics of imperfection. Can our imperfect art still stand proudly alongside its more graceful brothers—such as painting, poetry, the novel—in the realm of aesthetic beauty?

Clearly any set of aesthetic standards which seek perfection or near-perfection in the work of art will find little to praise in jazz. Yet this approach, however prevalent, is not the only valid way of evaluating works of art. A contrasting, if not complementary attitude looks not at the art in isolation but in relation to the artist who created it; it asks whether that work is expressive of the artist, whether it reflects his own unique and incommensurable perspective on his art, whether it makes a statement without which the world would be in some small way, a lesser place. This, I believe, is precisely the attitude towards art that delights in jazz. We enjoy improvisation because we take enormous satisfaction in seeing what a great musical mind can create spontaneously. We are interested in what the artist can do, given the constraints of his art. We evaluate Louis Armstrong or Charlie Parker not by comparing them with Beethoven or Mozart but by comparing them with other musicians working under similar constraints, and our notions of excellence in jazz thus depend on our understanding of the abilities of individual artists and not on our perception of perfection in the work of art. In short, we are interested in the finished product (the improvisation) not as an autonomous object but as the creation of a specific person. When we listen to Charlie Parker's records we take delight in probing the depths of his abilities as an artist, and even his failures interest us because they tell us about the musician who created them.

This, for better or worse, goes against the grain of many current attitudes towards art. The dogmatic criticism now practiced in many of the other arts is completely antithetical to this approach to jazz; it fixates on the art and not on the artist. The paradigm of the now dominant view is "deconstructive" criticism in which the work of art is viewed as totally divorced from the individual who created it. With this autonomy of the work of art, the artist's intentions in creating art are no longer of interest. Implicit in much earlier art criticism was the belief that it is permissible to interpret the work in ways the author never envisaged (this belief is at the root of Freudian and Marxist interpretations of art), but with "deconstruction" and the various other dehumanized approaches to art, the artist has completely disappeared—he is not even given the dubious honor of being psychoanalyzed. What we are left with is the bare work of art itself.

In this light, any defense of jazz based upon its ethos of individualism is bound to appear anachronistic. It focuses attention on the individual at the very same time that he seems to have fallen out of favor with most critics and philosophers of art (and not only there: the last few decades have witnessed an attack on the individual in fields as disparate as sociology, history, anthropology, the theory of meaning, linguistics, the history of science, and psychoanalysis). An aesthetic based on the individual artist has always bothered many by its extreme implications. How many of us would agree with John Ruskin's assertion that Gothic art is superior to other types of art, despite technical imperfections, because it gave greater scope to the creativity of the individual artist? Such a radically individualistic aesthetic has dangers of its own, but to a certain extent Ruskin is worth taking seriously: He calls attention to a simple, yet easily neglected fact, namely that art exists not in isolation but rather as the product of an artist. Such a truth may temporarily elude the dispassionate spectator at an art museum or the reader of a novel, but it is ever present to those in attendance at a jazz performance. In its own odd way, jazz has perhaps the most firm emphasis on individualism of all the arts.

Traditional approaches to aesthetics which search for Platonic ideals of art—which often present high culture as the consumption of polished and perfected "masterpieces"—are not without their merits. An appreciation of the human, and hence imperfect element of art could, however, serve to counter the obvious excesses of such a critical attitude pursued in isolation. The viewer of art, whether critic or spectator, can and should be more than a mere consumer of impersonal objects—he can legitimately attend both to the realities of the work of art as well as to the creative act which produced it.

Thus, an aesthetics of imperfection, one which accepts this human element in art, may not be restricted to jazz, but may be valuable in shaping our attitudes towards other artistic disciplines. Such an attitude, like jazz itself, is bound to seem peculiar in the light of recent intellectual trends. Yet by confronting the apparent imperfections of jazz, we may come to find that these so-called peculiarities are the common ground of all artistic endeavors. Our interest in the creative artist, far from being an immature obsession with cultural heroes, may lie at the heart of our appreciation of even the most disinterested and most perfect art.

IV

Neoclassicism

in Jazz

> To give oneself a code of laws is itself the highest form of freedom.
>
> MARTIN HEIDEGGER

I

Three revolutionary waves have passed over the landscape of jazz during its brief history, each leaving in its wake a radically changed musical environment.

The first transformation came only a few years after the initial appearance of jazz recordings in 1917. Under the powerful influence of Louis Armstrong, jazz developed into a more highly individualistic art form—one that emphasized and idealized the role of the individual soloist. The structured ensemble sound of earlier "classic" New Orleans jazz gave way to a looser, more free-form style of playing in which the improvisational element was dominant.

At the same time jazz developed what was probably its first "cult of personality." Armstrong gained a personal following that was to spread beyond the confines of New Orleans and eventually across the Atlantic Ocean; in its own way it anticipated the increasingly obsessive and introverted reception given by the jazz community to later artists such as Charlie Parker and John Coltrane. In addition, other artists of early jazz became the subject of posthumous idolization. Buddy Bolden, the first significant jazz trumpeter, was mentioned in print only once during his life—and that not for any musical reason but because he was arrested. But Bolden was elevated to a figure of mythic proportions after his death. Bix Beiderbecke, who like Bolden passed away in 1931, similarly acquired legendary status only after his tragic early death. The romanticization of the jazz musician which began with Armstrong clearly shaped both the future direction of the music as well as the perception of what had come before.

The second wave of change in jazz occurred during the 1940s, spurred by the innovations of the beboppers. Their impact, from a purely musical standpoint, was even more far-reaching than Armstrong's: the harmonic, rhythmic, melodic, and compositional aspects of jazz underwent a major reformulation—so much so that many contested whether the end result could still be classified as jazz. Yet, beyond the musicological impact, jazz was subject to an equally profound cultural change. For perhaps the first time, the jazz musician became enormously self-conscious of his role as artist. No longer content to view himself as a mere musician or entertainer, the jazz performer became more and more isolated from the world of popular music and increasingly aligned himself with the traditions and trappings of high culture.

Charlie Parker, the most creative and innovative of the beboppers, was the focal point for these changes. Well aware of his debt to earlier jazz saxophonists such as Lester Young, Johnny Hodges, and Benny Carter, Parker was also cognizant of a "spiritual" if not musical relationship with classical modernists such as Stravinsky, Bartók, and Hindemith. This alternate lineage showed up in strange and subtle ways: on gigs he would often summon his band to the stage by playing an extract from Hindemith; at his daughter Pree's funeral he asked that the music of Bartók be played; towards the end of his own life he approached the contemporary classical composer Edgar Varese requesting that Varese give him composition lessons. Parker's use of string orchestra accompaniment for his recordings and performances was another outgrowth of this desire to reconcile his jazz playing with the traditions of "serious" music. The "Bird with Strings" format met with only a lukewarm response from many jazz critics and fans, yet Parker was to cite his recording of "Just Friends" with strings as his personal favorite among his many releases. A host of later jazz artists—including Clifford Brown, Oscar Peterson, Bill Evans, Art Pepper, and, most recently, Wynton Marsalis—have followed Parker's lead in recording orchestral albums which have been perhaps personally gratifying but scarcely more successful from a critical standpoint.

A subtle but perhaps more important change in attitudes accompanied this new self-consciousness of the jazz musician. This was the view that jazz, as one of the serious arts, must progress or advance with each new generation of musicians. John Coltrane candidly observed to a *Downbeat* interviewer in 1960: "I want to progress, but I don't want to go so far out that I can't see what others are doing."[1] Coltrane's view, typical of so many jazz musicians of his era, would have been inconceivable in jazz a few decades earlier. This is not to say that previous musicians had not tried to be innovative. Indeed they had. But previous innovation was more focused on developing an individual and unique sound, whereas now musicians felt compelled to transform the art form by their contribution. The very emergence of the term "modern jazz" to describe this musical movement was indicative of a new mentality, one in which traditions were viewed as obstacles to be overcome or discarded.

The idea that art should *progress* like science is a rather extraordinary one, no matter how much artists and critics alike may have come to take it for granted. By an odd set of circumstances, this belief in progress has gained force in the world of art while, at the same time, being discredited in the world of science under the attacks of influential thinkers such as Thomas Kuhn and Paul Feyerabend. In the world of modern jazz, the desire to be "progressive" continues to motivate an enormous number of musicians and non-musicians. Thus, an exceptionally talented and expressive artist such as trumpeter Wynton Marsalis has been frequently taken to task for not progressing beyond existing jazz conventions; on the other extreme, an equally brilliant trumpeter, Miles Davis, has obviously felt driven to change the style of his music from time to time in order to remain at the forefront of jazz—in the 1940s when bebop was in vogue, Miles was a bebopper; in the 1950s, when the cool school emerged, Miles was at the forefront of the movement; in the 1960s Miles led one of the finest bands in mainstream jazz; later in the decade and throughout the 1970s Miles employed electric instruments and became a prominent exponent of jazz fusion music; in the 1980s Miles began recording the music of pop stars Michael Jackson and Cyndi Lauper. It is hard to conceive of a pre-World War II jazz artist displaying the same obsessive interest in being "progressive"; previous musicians such as Louis Armstrong or Duke Ellington certainly experimented and evolved during their early years, but when they achieved techniques that worked for them, they were not hesitant to use them year after year, decade after decade. The beboppers not only displaced the music of these earlier artists but, perhaps inadvertently, had an even greater impact in discrediting their implicit notion that art should be an expression and not necessarily a progression.

With this change in aesthetic, bebop sowed the seeds of its own destruction. The new ethos demanded that the prevailing norm be displaced, and the result was the third wave of change to disrupt the course of jazz. Still in its infancy, bebop was challenged by new heirs to the throne. The cool school, the funk school, and, most notably, the *avant-garde* school all borrowed the bebop advocacy of modernism in their attempts to establish a new paradigm for jazz. Instead of a clear succession of power, a fragmentation of styles ensued and has persisted until the present day. The post-modern era in jazz has thus witnessed a proliferation of schools and styles unprecedented in the music's history.

This fragmentation has brought with it its benefits as well as its costs. The main benefit has been a diversity of musical expression which is truly exciting. The varied range of innovative projects and performances of the past three decades has made the jazz scene one of the most fertile areas of all the arts. The costs of this fragmentation, however, are not insignificant. The abundance of schools and styles has led to the all but complete disappearance of a common language, a common set of standards, a shared notion of good and bad. In the absence of these things, the continued health of the art form lies in doubt. The benefits of pluralism threaten to collapse into the uncertainties of relativism.

II

Even in the earliest jazz, with its emphasis on ensemble playing, the incipient individualism of the art form was plainly evident. Nowhere is this seen more clearly than in the individual solo breaks which were crucial in maintaining the momentum and intensity of the jazz performance. The break, much like the cadenza in a classical concerto, allowed the individual soloist to stand out against the background of the ensemble. The break phrase would be an improvised motif of determinate length—usually one or two bars—played by a single soloist in isolation from the band. Its "hook" was provided by the striking and immediate contrast of an individual voice against the preceding ensemble sound.

As Gunther Schuller points out, in his seminal study *Early Jazz*, this device can be seen in an embryonic form in early ragtime compositions, for example Scott Joplin's 1901 piece "The Easy Winners."[2] Other commentators have traced it back even earlier to call-and-response patterns found in African music. Jelly Roll Morton, in one of his few attempts to be specific in enunciating his musical philosophy, insisted that the solo break was the essence of early jazz. He told ethnomusicologist Alan Lomax:

> Without breaks and without clean breaks, and without beautiful ideas in breaks, you don't even need to think about anything else, you haven't got a jazz band and you can't play jazz. Even if a tune haven't got a break in it, it's always necessary to arrange some kind of spot to make a break.[3]

True to form, Morton takes credit for the introduction of this device:

> A break, itself, is like a musical surprise which didn't come in until I originated the idea of jazz.[4]

Although Morton's claim of originator can be challenged—and it is worth noting that he also insisted that he was the first scat singer, the first to use the term "jazz," the first master of ceremonies, the first to record the washboard, and the first to use brushes (actually, in Morton's case, flyswatters) on drums—few can deny the ingenuity with which he incorpo-

rated breaks. In his hands they were indeed a "musical surprise" serving to release the tension built up by the preceding
ensemble passages. Morton's 1926 recording of the "Sidewalk
Blues" is an early example of this device at its best. With a
striking ten-bar introduction Morton sets the tone for the
whole composition: two bars of piano solo are followed by
two-bar breaks for each of the lead instruments—trombone,
cornet, and clarinet—finally followed by two bars of classic
New Orleans ensemble playing. This compact presentation
of each of the band members leads into a twelve-bar stop-time
chorus featuring the cornet player George Mitchell and using
the band for accompaniment only on beats two and four—
essentially conveying the feeling of a series of musical breaks.
A contrasting melody played by the ensemble leads into another stop-time chorus featuring, this time, clarinet player
Omar Simeon. The piece then modulates into a third melody
which is played twice before the piece comes to a close. Much
of the success of the "Sidewalk Blues" stems from the clever
use of these breaks and from the variety they lend to the composition. Working with only the most limited musical palette,
Morton anticipates Ellington in his ability to bring an enormous amount of instrumental activity into the confines of a
three-minute composition.

It is only a slight exaggeration to see the development of
jazz soloing as an extension of the early tradition of jazz
breaks. The break, like the solo in later jazz, was seen as an
opportunity for the musician to make a personal statement.
The earliest jazz musicians were judged by their ability to take
a break just as modern jazz artists are gauged by their strengths
as soloists. In fact, much of the early jazz vocabulary was developed by artists taking greater and greater rhythmic and melodic liberties in their breaks. This growth can be seen by
comparing, for example, King Oliver's break in his 1924 re-

cording of "Construction Gang" with Louis Armstrong's use of breaks on his 1927 version of "Potato Head Blues." Although only three years separate the two recordings, the contrast between the two soloists could hardly be more striking. Towards the end of "Construction Gang" Oliver takes an ambitious double-time break which, in its own way, foreshadows the later work of Armstrong; but Oliver is unable to achieve what he attempts—he loses the rhythmic feel of the passage halfway through and stumbles around the beat until the other musicians come back in. With Armstrong, in contrast, one finds a sureness in handling rhythms which previous jazz soloists simply did not have. The kinds of phrases Oliver stumbled over are executed by Armstrong with ease.

The two-bar break became much less common in later jazz. Some viewed it as an overworked device which, in many contexts, smacked of cliche. But though it ceased to have the importance for modernists that it held for Morton and his contemporaries, it nonetheless was the first step in a process of development that continued on through the modern period: a process that placed an ever increasing emphasis on the individual soloist and placed in relief jazz's rich heritage as ensemble music.

Each generation of jazz innovators has helped to further this tendency towards musical individualism. In the 1940s the beboppers reduced ensemble passages to a minimum and expanded the scope of the improvisational element. Two decades later John Coltrane legitimized solos of previously unheard-of length—forty minutes or longer devoted to a single improvisation. Today the *avant-garde* movement delights in lengthy solo performances by instruments once thought to be incapable of sustaining interest without a supporting group—saxophonist, bassist, drummer now stand alone, sufficient unto themselves. The days are long gone when a jazz fan would savor every note of an eight- or sixteen-bar solo of, say, a Lester Young or Teddy Wilson. Indeed jazz now threatens to collapse under the weight of its own excesses.

III

All these dramatic changes in jazz, with all their attendant vices and virtues, reached a culmination in the figure of John Coltrane. No other musician of the postwar era more closely exemplified the forces of change which were shaping the directions of the music. The contradictions which many observers saw in Coltrane were perhaps only the latent contradictions in modern jazz made manifest.

Born in September 1926 in Hamlet, North Carolina, Coltrane was the son of a tailor who played the violin, ukulele, and clarinet. Coltrane was given a school clarinet at age twelve. By the time he moved to Philadelphia in 1944, he was also playing the alto saxophone. In Philadelphia Coltrane began studying music at the Ornstein School and Granoff Studios. After a period in the Navy, during which he played with the Navy band, Coltrane returned to Philadelphia and began working with a number of local bands. When he joined Eddie "Cleanhead" Vinson's band in 1947, he switched to the tenor saxophone, the instrument on which he was to rise to fame.

After successive stints with Dizzy Gillespie, Earl Bostic, and Johnny Hodges, Coltrane achieved his first measure of real notoriety in 1955 when he joined the Miles Davis Band. A six-month stay with Thelonious Monk's group in 1957 broadened his harmonic perspective and gave him exposure with another of modern jazz's most visible exponents. By the time he returned to Davis in late 1957, Coltrane was already tagged as one of the emerging stars of jazz. He was "an angry young tenor" who was going to make his mark on the jazz world.

At first glance, Coltrane did not seem to fit the bill for future superstardom. Teo Macero, who produced the historic "Kind of Blue" session, remarks: "All I remember about Coltrane, besides his music, was that he was a very sweet guy. He'd smile like a little boy when Miles would play something he liked."[5] Art Blakey recalls an early encounter with Coltrane as follows:

> I played drums on the *Monk's Music* album for Riverside, where Monk expanded his group to a septet, with both Coleman Hawkins and John Coltrane on tenor. Naturally, Monk wrote all the music, but Hawk was having trouble reading it, so he asked Monk to explain it to both Trane and himself. Monk said to Hawk, "You're the great Coleman Hawkins, right? You're the guy who invented the tenor saxophone, right?" Hawk agreed. Then Monk said to Trane, "You're the great John Coltrane, right?" Trane blushed, and mumbled, "Aw . . . I'm not so great." Then Monk said to both of them, "You both play saxophone, right?" They nodded. "Well, the music is on the horn. Between the two of you, you should be able to find it."[6]

Certainly for a growing number of jazz fans he was, in fact, the "great John Coltrane." They viewed him as the heir apparent to Charlie Parker—and rightly so: his playing was the logical, and perhaps final, extension of Parker's innovations. It displayed an awe-inspiring virtuosity and driving intensity that both borrowed from the conventions of bebop while at the same time going beyond them. From the time he joined Monk in 1957 to the time of his death from a liver ailment a decade later, Coltrane's musical prowess brought him to the forefront of jazz, and made it possible for him to gain a following which eventually surpassed even Parker's in its dedication and obsessiveness. His popularity continued unabated, and in many ways grew, after his untimely passing; so much so, that this soft-spoken saxophonist from North Carolina remains today a cult figure of almost legendary stature.

During this same period Coltrane changed styles more frequently than some saxophonists change reeds. Initially Coltrane experimented with increasingly complex harmonic structures—an approach which reached its apotheosis with his virtuosic performances on his 1959 *Giant Steps* recording. A second and somewhat overlapping period saw Coltrane adapt Miles's modal approach and experiment with the superimposition of a variety of scales and rhythms over fairly static harmonies. From 1965 until his death Coltrane's playing became freer and more daring, at times moving into atonality. Over and above these pronounced stylistic changes were occasional forays into more traditional approaches: a collaboration with Duke Ellington, an album with vocalist Johnny Hartman, an album of ballads. In general one sensed the restlessness and constant striving of an exceptional musical mind.

Yet the words of praise were far from unanimous. This unsettled and unsettling musical presence was viewed with suspicion by many members of the jazz establishment. In many ways Coltrane's stormy reception by jazz critics and fans was a re-enactment of the response the beboppers received two decades earlier. Critic John Wilson echoed the sentiments of many when he wrote that Coltrane "often plays his tenor sax as if he were determined to blow it apart, but his desparate attacks almost invariably lead nowhere." Others were perceived by Coltrane's defenders as damning with faint praise: Whitney Balliett, for example, writing in the *New Yorker*, lauded Coltrane for demonstrating that "ugliness like life, can be beautiful." The English poet and jazz critic Philip Larkin expressed a similar view, although perhaps more bluntly, when he claimed that with Coltrane "jazz started to be *ugly on pur-pose.*"[7]

These voices of dissent, however, could hardly match the fervor of Coltrane's supporters. Perhaps "disciples" would be the more appropriate word—indeed the Coltrane cult had all the markings of a charismatic religious movement. Critic Frank Kofsky expressed a view by no means limited to himself when he wrote: "I am not a religious person, but John Coltrane was the one man whom I worshipped as a saint or even a god."[8] Kofsky took a decidedly more secular approach when, in November 1964, he voted for Coltrane for Vice President of the United States (Malcolm X was his choice for President). Kofsky's reaction, however, must be seen as mild compared to the more overtly theistic approach of San Franciscan Bishop Ramakrishna King Haqq. After hearing Coltrane play in 1965, Haqq founded the One Mind Temple Evolutionary Church of Christ; according to Haqq, members of his church view Coltrane as "the will of God . . . the incarnation truth."[9] As part of the John Coltrane Human Outreach Program the church members "bake bread, put Coltrane's picture on it and call it our daily bread, which we distribute to schools. When we put the image of John Coltrane on a shirt it is like a prayer cloth."

Several years ago Alice Coltrane, the musician's widow, launched a $7.5 million suit to stop what she views as the exploitation of Coltrane's name. Haqq's response was to the point: "Was it ever necessary," he asked "to ask Mother Mary to use Jesus' name?"

IV

Drawing parallels between stages in jazz's development and periods in the evolution of other arts is, at best, a questionable

endeavor. Yet the pronounced obsession with individual artists which has characterized the reactions of jazz fans, critics,
and even musicians at least since the time of Louis Armstrong—reaching its peak with the figure of John Coltrane—
can perhaps be best understood as the outgrowth of a temperament which is essentially "romantic" in nature.

Romanticism, with its idealization of the expressive artist,
created a new aesthetic vocabulary in the late eighteenth and
nineteenth century—one that fixated on the act of artistic production; one that glorified the passing moment of artistic inspiration as a secular epiphany; one in which the artist often
became more important than what he created. In many instances the artist's life actually became, in his eyes and in the
eyes of others, itself a work of art. With Byron, Wordsworth,
Keats, Goethe, Wagner, and many of their contemporaries,
biography and aesthetics begin to coalesce. The term "romanticism" has become worn with use, and, as more than one
critic has advocated, much might be gained by discarding it
entirely. Yet, as William Thrall has noted, "viewed in philosophical terms, romanticism does have a fairly definite meaning."[10] It designates a view of the world "which tends to see
the individual at the very center of all life and all experience,
and it places him, therefore, at the center of art." This aesthetic sensibility was often seen as having a special affinity
with the musical arts. As M. H. Abrams has noted, the German critics in particular saw

> music as the apex and norm of the pure and nonrepre-
> sentative expression of spirit and feeling against which to
> measure the relative expressiveness of all other art forms
> . . . [I]nquiry into the neo-representative character of
> music joined with many collateral influences to strain and
> shatter the frame of neo-classic theory, and to reorient all
> critical discussion toward the new magnetic north of the
> expressive and creative artist.[11]

The inherent romanticist elements in music are realized with particular force in jazz. In no other area of creative endeavor is there so little distance between the artist and his work of art. In the spontaneous act of improvisation, the artist has no opportunity to give his music a separate existence, to revise it, to reconsider it, to mull over it. The notion of the autonomous work of art—so fashionable in recent intellectual circles—has no place in jazz. Jazz music lives and dies in the moment of performance, and in that moment the musician *is* his music. His improvisation is the purest expression possible of the artist's emotions and feelings, and it is a purity which is only heightened by the absence of the spoken word. The German romanticist Novalis, arguing for the primacy of the musical arts, wrote towards the close of the eighteenth century: "The musician takes the essence of his art out of himself—and not the slightest suspicion of imitation can befall him."[12]

With his *a cappella* introduction to the *West End Blues,* Louis Armstrong ushered in a period of romanticism in jazz which has become, if anything, more pronounced with the passage of time. The increasingly individualistic nature of the music, the obsessive reactions of the jazz world to figures such as Parker or Coltrane, the almost complete breakdown of barriers between the artist and his work of art—all these legacies of Armstrong are the clear signs of an aesthetic sensibility which is essentially romanticist in character.

The benefits of such a musical environment are unmistakable. Jazz, as a community of creative individuals, fosters a pluralism which is healthy for the art form as a whole. It lacks the embedded institutions of the other arts, yet a stronger emphasis on group norms, exercised perhaps through academia or other mechanisms of standardization, would probably have stifled some of jazz's greatest talents. One could not imagine a Charles Mingus or a Thelonious Monk thriving in an environment in which artistic success depended on access to fellowships, government grants, academic appointments, and the like.

The benefits of jazz's pluralism, however, have not been achieved without a price. The attendant fragmentation of the jazz community has led to a lack of cohesion among practitioners, an absence of institutions for preserving and passing on the music's traditions, and, perhaps worst of all, a steady erosion of generally accepted critical standards which define what is good and bad in the music. Without the latter, musicians—as well as listeners and critics—may find their isolation only growing. The lack of common standards and a common musical vocabulary has exacerbated the collapse of the jazz world into countless schools and tendencies, each unable to communicate with those outside of its own small world.

Jazz has become, in effect, a music of perpetual romanticism The jazz world has always exhibited a manic quality in which the music's inherent vitality threatened to run away with itself. Today this strain is more dominant than ever before. By contrast, the powerful broadening and unifying influence of an Armstrong, an Ellington, a Parker is now apparently a thing of the past.

V

Within this pervasive aesthetic of emotional excess, however, a handful of musicians have tried to temper the music's natural impulse towards self-indulgence. They have created music of restraint, of control, of economy. These are the neoclassicists of jazz. Like neoclassical artists in other arts, they attempt to pare away the excesses of previous generations to reveal an art that is pristine and timeless. Their paradigm is the sculptor, whose work emerges from sharply cut and precisely defined lines, and whose warmth of expression is tempered by the cool, distant, and unforgiving medium with which he works. The neoclassicist recognizes that self-restraint is the essence of artistic style. A style which includes everything ceases to be a style—it has become an encyclopedia of techniques. The artist who embraces all of these techniques has, by the same token, reduced himself to a mere craftsman. Art begins only when some techniques are favored, others discarded.

Jazz, for these artists, is not just a music of possibilities, but rather a music of *constrained* possibilities. The temptation towards all-inclusiveness may have ruined more talent than all of the more publicized vices of the musician's life. Certainly when artistic norms collapse—as in our own day—the great artist must impose contraints upon himself. He must reject on his own what others are content to let go by.

Neoclassicism in jazz is not restricted to a specific time period or geographical area. Artists as different as Lester Young, Wes Montgomery, Bill Evans, Count Basie, Stan Getz, John Lewis, Miles Davis, and Paul Desmond can be included in its ranks, although under almost any circumstances the neoclassicist is part of a minority that distances itself from the more frenetic tradition of romanticism which permeates jazz. Thus the neoclassicist may appear to be perpetually out of fashion, a lone voice in the jazz world.

Jazz, in the hands of a neoclassicist, is a music of balance, of care, of restraint. With an unabashed lyricism and a subtle sense of formal structure, the neoclassicist displays his affinity for jazz's rich tradition of vocal music. The most successful collaborations of jazz singers and instrumentalists—the Billie Holiday/Lester Young recordings come immediately to mind— have more often than not been a part of this neoclassical heritage.

Yet the neoclassicist can often be distinguished not so much by his positive virtues as by what he excludes. Some pundit once remarked that the most telling thing about Jane Austen was that she never mentioned the French Revolution in her writings. A similar perspective, it seems, could be applied fruitfully to the study of musicians. Indeed one of the most striking characteristics of recent jazz in the romantic tradition is its all-inclusiveness. It attempts to encompass the whole musical world, from Third World folk music to the twelve-tone row. Neoclassicism, in contrast, is a music of exclusion, of omission.

VI

In the case of saxophonist Paul Desmond, one never needed to look far to find these omissions. The bebop cliches, the obsession with playing fast, the memorized licks which characterized jazz saxophone playing in the post-Charlie Parker era—all of these were noticeably absent in Desmond's music. As Dave Brubeck once mentioned, with no slight intended: "Paul's big contribution is going to be that he *didn't* copy Charlie Parker."[13]

A comparison between Desmond and his contemporary Charlie Parker is illuminating. Parker, perhaps the most brilliant improviser in the history of jazz, was at his best when the tempo was fast and the chord structure was complex: his virtuosity delighted in musical obstacle courses such as "Ko-Ko" or "The Hymn." Desmond, in contrast, seldom played at very fast tempos, and when he did one sensed that it was done unwillingly. Not that his technique was not equal to the task; rather it was Desmond's overriding concern with creating a melodic and thematically organized improvisation that led him to eschew the facile glibness of many of the beboppers. Unlike the less talented descendants of Parker who followed a credo of "let your fingers do the walking," Desmond played a thinking man's jazz with solos that often made punning reference to other compositions and improvisations. On an early recording of "You Go to My Head," for example, Desmond inserts a quote from a Charlie Parker blues in the midst of a most un-Parker-like passage. In other contexts he would incorporate long extracts from Chet Baker or Gerry Mulligan solos into his own improvisations.

Desmond was born less euphoniously as Paul Emil Breitenfeld on November 15, 1924, in San Francisco. His father was once an organist for silent movies and later an arranger. Paul began studying clarinet in 1936 while at San Francisco Polytechnic High School, and continued with it until 1943 when he switched to the alto saxophone. That same year he went into the Army and spent the next three years in San Francisco as part of the 253rd AGF band. "It was a great way to spend the war," Desmond later remarked. "We expected to get shipped out every month, but it never happened. Somewhere in Washington our file must still be on the floor under a desk somewhere."[14] After leaving the Army, Desmond played briefly with the bands of Jack Fina and Alvino Rey before joining forces with Dave Brubeck in 1951, a collaboration that would continue for over a quarter of a century.

At some point during this period, Desmond discarded the name Breitenfeld for his more manageable stage name. He claimed that he came upon the name Desmond while paging through a phone book. The remark is appropriate: for an improvising artist such as Desmond, the spontaneous, spur-of-the-moment decision is the basis of all he does. And Desmond, more than most, let the philosophy of improvisation govern much of his life outside of music. His casual attitude went beyond the choice of a name. At its worst it encouraged a pronounced habit of procrastination, and Desmond was a procrastinator of almost legendary proportions. For years he spoke of writing a book about his experiences with the Dave Brubeck Quartet. Only the title (*How Many of You Are There in the Quartet?*—according to Desmond, a favorite question of stewardesses) and one very funny chapter ever emerged.[15] Among his other intended projects was an album in which he planned to play each song in the style of a different alto player.

Perhaps the latter idea was only offered as a joke. With Desmond one could never tell. He once told an interviewer that he wanted his alto to sound like a very dry martini; whether his music attained this lofty goal is open to discussion, but of the dryness of his humor there can be no dispute. The humor figured prominently in his music—a rarity in modern jazz, where the artists' self-conscious seriousness and the concert hall atmosphere of even nightclub performances casts a sombre aura over most of the music. As his close friend, jazz critic Nat Hentoff wrote:

> At times Paul was the wittiest of improvisers. His ear was extraordinarily quick and true, his mind moved with eerie swiftness. He could take a phrase that someone had played earlier or a musical reference that a friend in the audience would understand and insert it into his solo. He'd build on that phrase until he had turned it inside out and seven other ways. Usually this kind of quoting is trickery, but Paul made it cohere. In his music, as in his life, the absurd cohabited with the familiar.[16]

For much of his twenty-six-year career, Desmond found his musical skills overshadowed by the work of his longtime friend and collaborator Dave Brubeck. Brubeck, who studied with Darius Milhaud in the late 1940s, was a pioneer in the synthesis of jazz and classical music—his piano work featured dense harmonies, a studied sense of rhythm, and the use of elements seemingly alien to jazz such as the twelve-tone row and odd time signatures. Yet Desmond was the unsung hero of the Brubeck Quartet; as much as the group's leader, Desmond was instrumental in shaping the ensemble's distinctive sound. His lyrical tone was immediately identifiable, and his ingenious compositions (most notably the group's biggest hit "Take Five") were an important part of the band's repertoire. Although not a student of Milhaud's, Desmond was involved with Brubeck's experimental work from the start. His affinity for classical music was also revealed in other ways—most markedly in his intonation, which was remarkably pure, especially when contrasted with the "dirtier" sound favored by many of his contemporaries.

In the midst of a period in which cool jazz and West Coast jazz were increasingly the scorn of jazz critics, Desmond embraced both with a vengeance. Desmond was well aware of what passed as fashionable in jazz circles; commenting on Bud Shank, a fellow Californian (although one transplanted from Ohio), Desmond said: "I sympathize with him because I have the same problem in my occupation, which is the problem of one who is sort of raised in the atmosphere of cool jazz trying to sound hostile enough to be currently acceptable."[17] In another interview he elaborated: "The things I'm after musically are clarity, emotional communication on a not-too-obvious level, form in a chorus that doesn't hit you over the head but is there if you look for it, humor, and construction that sounds logical in an unexpected way. That and a good dependable high F-sharp and I'll be happy."[18]

The virtues Desmond enumerated are easy enough to list, but maddeningly difficult to attain. Desmond's dissatisfaction with his own playing frequently came to light in many of the interviews he gave over the years. As Lee Konitz, a contemporary who shares many similarities with Desmond, commented: "I feel that Paul has experienced greatness, and once this feeling of playing what you really hear has been felt by a player, it's difficult to settle for less than this."[19]

One senses that towards the end of his life Desmond came

closer than ever to realizing this goal. His last recordings reveal an artist who is at peace with himself and who knows with a dogged assurance what it is he wants to express. The ravages of lung cancer may have lessened his stamina and shorted his phrases, but if anything this led Desmond to be even more refined and thoughtful in his playing.

The sardonic humor, however, remained. One wonders what to make of the cover of *Live,* the last album he saw released. Desmond is pictured seated alone in a club at closing time—the chairs are stacked on the tables, and Desmond is packed to go with a suitcase, or perhaps his saxophone case, at his side. The artist is smoking a cigarette, although even then he must have known he had only a short time before lung cancer would take its final toll. Another detail: if one looks closely, one notices little skulls and crossbones on Desmond's suspenders. These details, combined with the album's ironic title and Desmond's grim smile, are powerfully unnerving. The music inside, however, is every bit as beautiful as the album's cover is morbid. His solo on "Wave" could be a textbook example of solo construction, each chorus outdoing the previous one in inventiveness and incisiveness. Elsewhere, on his own composition "Wendy" or in his closing chorus on "Manha de Carnival" Desmond plays as well as at any point in his career. This is the music of a master.

The end was approaching fast. His last appearance in a recording studio was for friend Chet Baker's debut album with the Horizon label. He had been slated to play on the entire album, but had the stamina to record just one track before begging leave to go home and rest. Although he had rarely played in the preceeding months, his tone was as pure as ever and his short haunting solo is as fitting a closing statement as any artist could wish to make.

His were the legacies of a man immersed in music. Desmond's piano, left to Bradley Cunningham, now graces Bradley's in New York, and has acquired a reputation as one of the finest nightclub pianos in jazz. His alto was left to Brubeck's son Michael, with whom he shared a special closeness. Yet these pale beside his legacy to jazz fans through his many records and a few—too few—short writings. Desmond, a West Coast musician at a time when that was virtually synonymous with being unfashionable, had his ashes scattered over Big Sur country near his birthplace in San Francisco.

VII

"In the Classical world," Oswald Spengler asserts at one point in his massive work *The Decline of the West,* "music was the art that failed."[20] Spengler perceived that other art forms, most notably sculpture and fresco painting, were better equipped to achieve the restraint (which Spengler, borrowing from Nietzsche, characterize as "Apollinian" restraint) inherent in classicism. Polyphonic music, by contrast, was not Apollinian but, in Spengler's terminology, "Faustian" art; it rejected all limitations and aspired towards the infinity of endless space. The Renaissance, viewed by most historians as a renewal of classical ideals, achieved this renewal, in Spengler's view, only in those rare moments when it "succeeded in achieving something wonderful that music could not reproduce,"[21] when it achieved, for example, the clarity of a Michelangelo sculpture. To the extent that a classical style re-emerged in the Renaissance, it was because it was the "one moment in the history of the West when sculpture ranked as the preeminent art."[22]

This dominance of sculpture was destined to be short-lived. Only for a few decades in Florence ("the only area where Classical and Western landscapes touched") was this Apollinian ideal revived. With Sandro Botticelli and Filippino Lippi, even with Leonardo da Vinci, one already senses a desire to go beyond the limitations of the human form; even when classical subjects are depicted, they are portrayed in a new manner, one in which the play of light and shade is as important as the human figure. Yet this new aspiration, one which sought the perfection of pure and unlimited space, would reach its culmination not in painting but in music. By the time of Haydn, Mozart, and Beethoven, Faustian music reigns supreme and sculpture is tolerated only as a minor art.

If, as Spengler suggests, *clarity* and *restraint* are especially difficult virtues for any music to achieve, how much more difficult must it be for jazz to possess these selfsame qualities. Jazz improvisation, by its very nature, tends towards apparent formlessness towards a breakdown of structural coherence, towards excess. The confusion of the layman on first encountering modern jazz, summed up perfectly by critic Martin Williams in the question "Where's the Melody?," is not just a sign of the outsider's characteristic "unhipness" but rather a telling recognition of the very essence of jazz. Under the pressure of spontaneous creation, the jazz artist has little opportunity to impose on his music the architectonic sense of order and balance that distinguishes the more leisurely constructed arts. As in Yeats' "The Second Coming": "Things fall apart; the centre cannot hold." The neoclassicist struggles against this inherent tendency in the music. Like the sculptor he goes against the grain of his medium, attempting to shore up a few fragments against the ruin and musical dissolution going on around him. As Paul Desmond succinctly put it, the improviser must "crawl out on a limb, set one line against another and try to match them, bring them closer together."[23]

These neoclassicists are jazz's true sculptors: the classicism they are trying to revive, however, is not that of antiquity; if anything, they are harking back to the restraint of "classic" New Orleans jazz, pre-Louis Armstrong. In, for example, the King Oliver recordings of the early twenties, the individual players aspired towards creating a coherent group sound in which the soloist was subservient to the ensemble; in the case of Jelly Roll Morton (anticipating in this regard the later work of Duke Ellington, Gil Evans, and John Lewis), the musicians were markedly concerned with doing justice to the composition. In either case, such examples of musical self-restraint became extremely rare as jazz evolved; composition and ensemble became increasingly subservient to the individual soloist, and almost any violation of taste became more or less acceptable so long as it contributed towards creating a virtuoso instrumental performance. In this changed musical environment the modern neoclassicist, with his emphasis on producing a coherent musical statement, is very much out of place. Though he plays a music which is much different from these early works of Jelly Roll Morton and King Oliver, there is a spiritual affinity nonetheless: both are striving for a balance and restraint which is often at odds with jazz's tendency towards extremes.

Former Oxford professor Edgar Wind, in his brilliant 1960 lectures later published as *Art and Anarchy*, suggests that art which relies primarily upon intensity runs special risks. "While mediocrity would tend in any style to weaken or destroy the aesthetic illusion," writes Wind, "mediocrity which claims to be intense has a peculiarly repulsive effect."[24] Wind obviously had no thought of modern jazz in mind when he made this observation, yet his remark is particularly apt when viewed in the context of contemporary improvised music. Over the past four decades, jazz artists have increasingly pursued this ideal of an intense and unrelenting art form. At its best—in, for example, the recordings of Charlie Parker or Dizzy Gillespie—such jazz can be extraordinarily exhilirating; but such successes are too often the exception rather than the rule. The far more frequent result of this institutionalized obsession with intensity is precisely the kind of repulsion which Wind describes. Perhaps it is this extreme adherence to the trappings of romanticism which has caused jazz, over the same four decades, to lose its once large popular audience while failing to gain a following in the highbrow cultural circles which are usually willing to embrace other areas of artistic endeavor.

The neoclassicist in jazz is less open to this particular kind of failing—yet he faces other, perhaps equally daunting difficulties in attempting to pursue his ideals. His endeavor to attain form in an environment which tends toward formlessness is bound to be accompanied by frustration and frequent failure. And even when the improviser is successful in his attempt to impose structure onto his playing, the subtlety of his achievement may well elude all but the most attentive listener. In comparison with the more striking and obvious virtues of jazz's romanticists—intensity, virtuosity, and, above all, emotional immediacy—the neoclassicist stresses the less salient attributes of understatement, restraint, and taste.

His may well be a losing battle. History is clearly on the side of the romanticist; the whole development of jazz has increased his sway over the music. To control jazz's inherent tendency towards excess is perhaps a Herculean task, beyond the scope of any of today's musicians. The struggle, however, may be worth it. A continuation of the dominant trend seems likely to inflict wounds from which jazz may never recover. Meanwhile the neoclassicist, in his lonely pursuit of form and order, has been left to seek an ideal of musical perfection—almost Platonic in nature—that contemporary jazz, in its fervor, appears to have given up long ago.

V

What Has Jazz to Do
with Aesthetics?

STUDENT: "If my landlady says a picture is lovely and I say it is hideous, we don't contradict one another."

WITTGENSTEIN: ". . . This is just the stupid kind of example which is given in philosophy, as if things like 'This is hideous,' 'This is lovely' were the only kinds of things ever said. . . . You might think Aesthetics is a science telling us what's beautiful—almost too ridiculous for words. I suppose it ought to include also what sort of coffee tastes well."

From student notes of Wittgenstein's lectures on aesthetics

I

The mystery of art lies not so much in its beauty or hideousness but in the fact that it should communicate with us at all. It is something approaching a miracle that a piece of canvas covered with paint or a succession of musical tones of set duration can communicate emotions and sensations of immense power, even when continents or centuries—or both—separate artist and audience. This communication, often achieved without the use of words, symbols, or other linguistic means, presents us with an enigma as great as any treated by the other philosophic disciplines. As such it is the proper starting point for any study of aesthetics.

The very prevalence of such artistic communication dulls our sense of its wonder. Our engagements with art, and especially with music, are so widespread and pervasive that we view its emotive power as far from unusual. It is taken for granted as an established fact of artistic discourse. Yet how can we account for this unusual kind of communication? What exactly is communicated? Feelings? Ideas? Impressions? Even casual consideration of the matter indicates that this is a type of communication unlike that which we encounter in our day-to-day relations with people. My conversations with a neighbor or co-worker may pose philosophical problems of their own (and, indeed, one cannot overestimate Analytic Philosophy's capacity for making everyday activities appear fraught with difficulty); yet such dialogues seem positively non-problematic when compared with the more indirect communication found in aesthetic encounters.

If, as I believe, the work of art serves as a mediator between artist and audience, such mediation is far from straightforward. Certainly the modern observer of, for example, a Fra Angelico fresco is not capable of recreating, or perhaps even imagining, the original mental state of the artist himself. Nor does he look at such a work with the pristine eyes of its first viewers. His "point of view" is largely a modern construction, profoundly shaped through acquaintance with innumerable later works of art with all their attendant refinements of perspective, coloring, detail, and so on. Even the physical aspect of the work he is viewing has undergone significant changes during the span of time since it was painted—fading, darkening, cracking, and the like. Hence the distinctive and somber colors so characteristic, for example, of the work of Rembrandt may be a result of environmental changes as much as they are signs of the artist's original conception. Or, as in the case of a work such as Leonardo da Vinci's *Last Supper,* centuries of undocumented "restoration" have added to the natural deterioration of the work, further amplifying the noise which separates artist and audience.

Yet, even in the face of these many obstacles, the modern observer often encounters something powerful and precious in his relationship with such works. His experience is such that he rebels against categorizing his responses as arbitrary or purely subjective, as based on mere whim or prejudice, as simply a personal reaction to an impersonal physical object. The work of art, for him, is distinguished from natural phenomena by its unmistakable status as a human product— otherwise, as Wittgenstein points out, aesthetics might as well concern itself with "what sort of coffee tastes well."[1] Through the work of art, *something* is communicated from artist to audience, even across an enormous span of time and across vast differences of culture and environment. The problem of this "something" is the fundamental problem of aesthetics.

II

At first glance it may seem unlikely that a study of jazz could have any special bearing on this topic. The very existence of aesthetics, as a branch of philosophy concerned with general principles of art, would appear to depend upon the possibility of treating the subject in a general way, unaffected by the idiosyncrasies of individual arts. By this standard, an aesthetics *of* jazz is as much an impossibility as a theory of literature derived from the study of a single novel. To the extent that precepts apply to one and only one art form, they

cease to be precepts of aesthetics. They become critical judgments or techniques of execution, both of which are far different, if not necessarily lesser things.

Therefore, the focus is not on an aesthetics *of* jazz, but
rather on aesthetics *and* jazz. For, though the nature of jazz
does not and cannot define aesthetics, it may well raise certain crucial issues which emerge less clearly in the study
of other arts. Jazz, in other words, may serve as a sort of
testing ground for principles that may later be applied to art
in general. Theories of aesthetics have rarely taken into account the eccentricities of improvised and spontaneous art,
and an examination of such art, best exemplified by jazz music, in the light of these theories reveals certain conflicts which
suggest that one or the other must go. Either jazz is not a true
art form or the aesthetic theory in question is invalid.

This conflict emerges even in preliminary definitions of
the nature of art, for example, in the question of whether
art is an activity or an object. When viewed as an object of
contemplation, jazz may well fail even the most basic tests
of aesthetic success. Created spontaneously as improvised
art, jazz lacks the more refined beauty of, for example, sculpture or architecture. Yet when judged as an activity, jazz
need make no apologies: the vitality and intensity of the
jazz performance can become almost hypnotic, captivating
both musician and audience in a fleeting and unique performance.

The salience of jazz's virtues when viewed as an activity
are due, at least partly, to its existence as a temporal art form.
It cannot be grasped entirely in an instant as is, arguably, the
case with many visual arts. In temporal arts such as music,
cinema, and dance, the role of activity is more apparent than
in the plastic arts, and any attempt to reduce the work to
a physical object is more easily resisted. An aesthetician, such
as Carl Dalhaus, who focuses on the musical arts, will usually

avoid any such clumsy reductionism.[2] Yet even here more than a few philosophers of art have dissented: some, like Nelson Goodman, minimize the central role of activity in music by arguing that the musical score, and not the performance, defines the work;[3] others, like Eduard Hanslick, or before him Immanuel Kant, view music as somehow suspect because its transitory nature detracts from the "pure act of contemplation which alone is the true and artistic method of listening."[4]

Jazz suffers considerably from either of these approaches. Whatever limitations which may be inherent in temporal arts are aggravated by jazz's unpremeditated method of artistic creation. Unlike other types of music, jazz cannot even point for justification to the musical score with its perfected, architectonic structures. If a Bach fugue, with all its polished and perfected melodic lines, is a lesser art according to Kant— "it merely plays with sensations"—how much less worthy of praise must be the jazz performance, with all the flaws and excesses of improvised art?

Hence, if our appreciation of a work of art were based on its attainment of certain specified standards of perfection, then jazz is likely to fare poorly when judged. At first blush, such an approach to art seems wholly justified. Certainly the very existence of aesthetics presupposes the existence of good art and bad art, and the simple fact that we apply the adjective "good" to the word "art" implies that the goodness is an attribute of the art. If we cannot look to the work of art for its goodness, where can we look?

Yet this approach takes what is essentially a *relationship* and treats it as though it were a *thing*. In the jargon of Marxism, the observer who has simplified the matter in this way has committed an error of *reification*. Although Marx, and after him Georg Lukacs, analyzed this as an economic phenomenon—in which relationships between individuals in a capitalist society were disguised as properties of commodities[5]—the same approach can be applied fruitfully to the study of art. The recent craze in art criticism for semiotics, structuralism, and deconstruction (much of it, quite ironically, from a Marxist perspective) takes precisely this kind of reified view of the work of art. The finished work is now conveniently divorced from the artist, whose intentions, thoughts, and aims can now, one is assured, be safely disregarded.

This attitude towards art, however fashionable it might be at the moment, is no recent addition to the aesthetic canon. At least as far back as Plato, thinkers have often tended towards viewing art as a thing apart, as an object of contemplation not describable in merely human terms. The work of art, for such thinkers, served as a representative of some higher ideal or spiritual reality. Neoplatonism, German Idealism, English Romanticism—each flirted with this approach in its own distinct way, the result being that the physical work of art itself—the painted canvas, the carved marble, the printed manuscript—was invested with a symbolic, if somewhat vague, importance which it could scarcely sustain. So much so that philosopher John Dewey was forced to exclaim: "By one of the ironic perversities that often attend the course of affairs, the existence of the works of art upon which formation of an esthetic theory depends has become an obstruction to theory about them."[6]

Jazz remains out of place in a culture that places such enormous emphasis on the physical object of art. Society's veneration for the artistic product is attested to by the existence of academies, galleries, concert halls, and museums, and though jazz is slowly coming to be similarly institutionalized, the process is by no means a smooth or promising one. Almost every aspect of the music rebels against such an approach—by nature it is ephemeral, spontaneous, and informal;

and by historical accident it is cut off from the elite classes and institutions which serve to certify "masterpieces." In this light, it is worth asking why jazz, for all its apparent flaws, has managed to attract a serious audience. What do they find in jazz that is not present in a more perfected manner in other types of music? For no matter what a jazz fan may claim, even the best improvised melody suffers by comparison with, for example, a Bach fugue. The conditions of its genesis defy such calculated perfection.

Our interest in jazz, it would seem, is less a matter of our interest in the perfection of the music, and more a result of our interest in the expressiveness of the musician. The jazz performance, perhaps more than any other kind of artistic event, allows the audience to confront the creative act. The opportunity to watch brilliant musical minds try to create something *ex nihilo* is obviously what draws the audience to the art form. These creations are judged accordingly: not by comparison with some Platonic ideal of perfection but by comparison with what other musicians can do under similar conditions. Our interest lies primarily in the artist and only secondarily in the art. The music is *his* music, the expression is *his* expression, and the success is his success just as the failure is his failure.

The question arises: Is this a valid way of approaching art? Or is it, rather, a type of aesthetic pandering, giving the audience the immediacy but not the substance of art? Can we justify such an interest in the artist, or does this "hero worship" obstruct us in evaluating the merits of his work? Must art stand alone, unaffected by merely human considerations?

III

A hypothetical example shows how deeply rooted is our interest in the human element of art.

Imagine the often cited situation of a group of chimpanzees sitting in a room with a number of typewriters. Given an infinite amount of time, these chimpanzees will eventually type an infinite amount of material—most of it unintelligible gibberish, but some minute portion of it making sense. An even smaller portion of it will represent, not just coherent writing, but literature of high quality.

But even if one of the chimpanzees managed to type out a play which, to an unknowing audience, was as good as Shakespeare's—even so, most of us, upon discovering the origin of the work, would feel vaguely uneasy about considering it as art. A happy circumstance?—yes! An entertaining drama?—certainly! But art? Not really. Our sensibility rebels against awarding the chimpanzee's play the label of art, just as one would refuse to consider a beautiful landscape or sunset, however breathtaking, as works of art. The inherent quality of the work is not the defining factor; otherwise all human products would fare poorly in comparison with the more perfected beauties of nature. Instead it is the human element, and its success or failure in finding expression, that is the basic aesthetic fact.

Let us examine a more reasonable example. Imagine a computer which has been programmed to compose musical works in any style. Even if the computer produced works stylistically and qualitatively indistinguishable from Mozart's, we would still be unwilling to consider them as comparable to the Austrian composer's pieces. The two are incommensurable. Mozart's works are artistic masterpieces, and the computer's output, however admirable, is something else entirely. The latter's perfection no more reflects on the composer's art than the existence of motor boats affects our judgement of how difficult it is to swim across the English Channel. Human achievement is a thing apart from mechanical or electronic achievement.

Thus, not only is our interest in the human element in art a justifiable concern, it is in fact a necessary concern. Standards of artistic success or failure are not absolute, measured against some Platonic ideal. They are empirical standards measured against the reality of what other artists in comparable situations have produced. This is not to imply that artistic creation is some type of athletic event—one in which competitors, operating under equal rules, vie for the laurel. The successful artist is not so much a victor over others as he is a victor over himself, mastering his often fragmented feelings and impressions and expressing them in a work which is uniquely his own. Art, in the words of the great modern aesthetician Benedetto Croce, is "expressive activity," and lives and dies by the success of that expression.[7]

IV

One day in the summer of 1947, painter Jackson Pollock took an extraordinarily daring step. He laid his canvas on the floor of the barn which served as his studio and, dispensing with brush and palette, began flinging house paint onto it. He would circle around the barn, applying paint from each direction; occasionally he would stop, unsure of how to continue, and hang the painting on the barn wall for a few days while he waited for the inspiration to finish it. This radical departure from accepted techniques would eventually become an established technique in its own right, but at the time Pollock was far from confident about the nature of his achievement. His concern was not, however, with the quality of his new paintings—that was a secondary issue. A different, more

basic question preoccupied him. Lee Krasner, Pollock's wife
and a fellow artist, recalls: "You know, Jackson used to grab
me by the arm, shaking, and ask 'Is this a painting?' Not a
good or bad painting—just was it a painting at all."[8]

In retrospect we can see that Pollock's dilemma stemmed
not from the physical works themselves. It was, rather, a
more recondite issue which troubled him. The question his
work posed, a question perhaps equally relevant today, was
whether the artistic act were more important than the artistic
work it produced. The essence of Pollock's abstract expressionism lie in its emphasis on the former at the expense of
the latter. The act of painting, the visceral sensation of flinging paint on canvas, was what such works celebrated. One's
view of the paintings in question would depend on how one
viewed the activity which produced them. What was needed
to "appreciate" them was not so much critical sensitivity and
taste, at least not initially, but something more basic: a notion of what constituted art.

Abstract expressionism and jazz shared an overlapping audience during much of the 1950s, and from this perspective
one can easily understand why. The hipsters who visited the
galleries and frequented the jazz clubs were, whether they
realized it or not, witnessing something similar in these two
superficially different environments. This was a similarity not
so much in medium or style but in philosophy. The distinc-
tiveness of jazz, much like that of Pollock's breakthrough in
1947, depended not so much on its existence as a different
kind of art, but on the fact that it embodied a whole different
attitude towards art. It required a different set of aesthetic
assumptions than did, say, a Bernini sculpture or a Mozart
string quartet. The question raised by both jazz and abstract
expressionism was the same: How does one judge performance art which emphasizes the performance more than the

art? Painting is not typically considered a performance art, yet Pollock's revolutionary approach could only be understood in that context: such works tried to capture the energy and vitality present in the moment of creation. In this regard they were strikingly similar to jazz, and though jazz has never been as controversial as Pollock's works, it too needs to justify itself against the criticism that its finished products cannot stand alone, separated from the forces that created them, as great works of art.

The implications of such a critique are for jazz quite profound. If, from one perspective, it appears hopelessly flawed, from another it is a paragon of artistic excellence. If we view art not as a class of perfected objects but as the foremost area for creative human expression, then the jazz experience is almost unique in its ability to convey that experience unadulterated by the intermediaries which separate artist and art in other disciplines. Similarly, jazz is largely uncorrupted by the trappings of high art, whose traces too often stultify this expressive activity in other areas and transform a once living art into a petrified and stylized artifact. The informality of jazz and of its usual settings, however damaging they have been to the music's claim to be taken seriously, keep it honest—painfully so—in this regard.

We have come a long way from the view, expressed succinctly by Hermann Weyl, that "beauty is bound up with symmetry."[9] At its extreme, such an attitude makes aesthetics into a branch of mathematics whose goal is to seek specific algebraic or geometric relationships, timeless in nature, by which a disinterested observer can evaluate all art—from the prehistoric to the post-modern. This belief in the aesthetic power of symmetry is deeply ingrained in Western culture and its lineage can be traced back to pre-Socratic times. It was such a dominant theme in medieval art that even the subject matter of sacred works would undergo change to meet its needs. As Umberto Eco has pointed out in his study *Art and Beauty in the Middle Ages:*

> The principle and criterion of symmetry, even in its most elementary forms, was rooted in the very instincts of the medieval soul. . . . [O]ften enough the requirements of symmetry modified the tradition, violating even the most ingrained beliefs and the most sacrosanct details. Thus, in a painting in Soisson we find that one of the Magi is omitted because a third figure would have destroyed the balance of the composition. Similarly, in Parma Cathedral we find St. Martin dividing his cloak with two beggars instead of one. In San Cugat del Valle's, in Catalonia, there are two Good Shepherds instead of one.[10]

The flowering of humanism during the Renaissance may have served to temper the more extreme versions of this faith in the underlying mathematical essence of art; nonetheless, the extraordinary interest in proportion and perspective among Renaissance artists revealed their basic acceptance of these earlier beliefs. Moreover, their image of the ideal "Renaissance man" blurred the distinction between the demands of scientific inquiry and artistic expression—works such as Benvenuto Cellini's autobiography or Leonardo da Vinci's notebooks demonstrated the amazing scope and potential of this new hybrid. For such artists, the expressive qualities of art could exist only within the confines of a balanced and tightly ordered perspective on their craft and on the universe as a whole.

The legacy of such earlier attitudes is evident in many of our contemporary suppositions about art. The persisting debate over art's formal qualities is but one example of a lingering hope that the creative art can be reduced to abstract rules derived from something approaching scientific inquiry. By implication, the human attributes of art, flawed as they are by being truly *human* products, can only *aspire* to this ideal of art as a class of perfected objects.

The devotees of jazz can find little solace in such beliefs. As a formal art, jazz has surprisingly little to offer: its excesses and deficiencies are only too apparent, and its small body of formal structures are mostly borrowed from other musical disciplines. Yet if it lacks the polished attributes of other, more staid arts, jazz still gives its audience something else, perhaps more precious, in exchange: it offers a rare glimpse into the creative act itself, and displays the extraordinary vitality that can only come from creative human efforts.

The contemporary scholar Frederick Turner has argued quite forcefully that performance art is the quintessential form of human artistic expression, not only for purely aesthetic reasons but because of its congruence with the very structure and evolution of the human brain.[11] The time-honored formulas of the traditional oral poets are, from this view, more powerful and satisfying than more formally complex works such as Spenser's *Faerie Queen* or than many of the richly ambiguous texts of modern literature. Even reading, at its best, may be a type of performance which, however ephemeral, gains strength from its particularities of time and place.

Jazz, as performance art *par excellence,* has little to apologize for from this perspective. Its unpolished beauty may, in fact, stand as a compelling argument for viewing art as a spiritual and expressive communication between artist and audience and not as a class of perfected objects. Ltke Prometheus, who brought fire from the gods to share with man, jazz can perhaps serve to carry art back from the unattainable world of divine perfection and bring it within the sphere of truly human endeavor.

VI

Boredom and Jazz

I like to be bored.   ANDY WARHOL

I

Few critics, one supposes, would share Andy Warhol's sentiments on boring art. In fact, surprisingly few major writers on art seem to have had much of anything to say on the subject of boredom. Audiences should be so lucky! Certainly as an empirical fact, "the Boring" is every bit as prevalent as "the Beautiful" or "the Sublime"—alas, perhaps even more prevalent. But in the world of art criticism, empirical reality seems to have been bested by the remnants of an ancient, but still lingering faith in aesthetics as a meditation on Platonic ideals of perfection. Boredom, along with the unfortunate flesh-and-blood viewer of boring art, has apparently been left behind in Plato's cave.

The popular arts have been the most open to accepting boredom as a possible, or even probable, audience reaction.

Television, for example, is frequently attacked for being boring—a proclamation all the more noteworthy coming, as it often does, from observers who spend a significant portion of their time in communion with major network programming. The makers of motion pictures are equally familiar with boredom and the impact it can have on an art form. A boring film may get glowing reviews, but box office receipts will reflect how well—or how poorly—it holds an audience's interest.

In contrast to the movie buff or the television viewer, the connoisseur of high culture is by no means so ready to be bored. At the exit of the concert hall, opera house, or art gallery, admissions of *ennui* are scarcely ever heard—although one suspects that even devotees of the highest culture, were their sincerest thoughts expressed aloud, would be voicing sentiments not far removed from those of their counterparts at the drive-in theater or in front of the television set. Even so, boredom is rarely mentioned on such occasions: the patrons of "serious" art, like the faithless visitors to a religious shrine, often prefer to pretend that their rote participation in an obscure ritual is, in fact, the celebration of something spiritual and profound. In such instances the "seriousness" is in them, and not in the art.

Jazz, at least in this respect, is closer to high art than to low art. That much—if not most—jazz is boring seems scarcely undeniable; given its extreme dependence on improvisation, jazz is more likely than other arts to ramble, to repeat, to bore. Even so, few of jazz's critics and commentators seem willing to apply the standard of boredom in evaluating a jazz performance. Other standards of evaluation may be applied—Is the work in question "progressive"? Is it sufficiently intense? Does it swing? Is it authentic? But what is perhaps the most obvious question is rarely asked: Does it sustain our interest? Is it *boring*? Is it *engaging*?

In this regard contemporary jazz has become remarkably

akin to the standard repertory arts. In the great repertory arts—in ballet, opera, and other classical music; to some extent in drama and the musical—the vast majority of performances are repetitions of past masterpieces rather than new creations. In such a cultural environment any suggestion that a work in question is boring is, to most people, an unacceptable criticism. These are *masterpieces,* one is reminded, and any deficiency is by necessity on the part of the audience and not the art. To the extent that high culture rejects boredom as an appropriate standard, it is due to the weight of centuries of masterpieces, next to which any one observer is a pitiful thing indeed.

The effects of the same attitude in jazz can be seen everywhere. Not only is jazz now treated as seriously as the repertory arts but it is in fact developing a repertory. In one respect it always had one: jazz musicians have often favored certain popular songs—George Gershwin's "I've Got Rhythm," Cole Porter's "Love for Sale," Harold Arlen's "Over the Rainbow," to cite just a few examples—to serve as a basis for improvisation. But recently a far more drastic change has taken place: the improvisations, the instrumentations, the arrangements of past jazz recordings are often recreated note for note in historical efforts to replicate the ensemble music of past masters such as Jelly Roll Morton, King Oliver, Louis Armstrong, or Duke Ellington. In less extreme cases groups will focus on merely the compositions of an artist and create their own improvisations—this has been done with the music of modern composers such as Charles Mingus, Tadd Dameron, or Thelonious Monk. On the other extreme are attempts to take the music of a Thelonious Monk or a Bill Evans and score it, for example, for string quartet. Jazz's aspiration to be a true repertory art is most clearly revealed in these often unusual musical products.

Such attempts to preserve jazz's past are, when viewed from

the historian's perspective, wholly admirable. Viewed from the perspective of a jazz fan, however, they take on a different aura. The essential elements of jazz—spontaneity, creativity, variety, surprise—may appear in these recreations in form but not in substance, and their arrival signals that the art form has undergone an important change, one in which the audience's natural relation to art—determined at the most basic level by whether they are bored or engaged by the work— is replaced by a "historically aware" appreciation of the work's significance. The result is music that is jazz-like without actually being jazz. Such efforts often bring with them historical accuracy alone, and not the improviser's spirited fancy.

II

These musical artifacts run counter to the culture of spontaneity which has dominated jazz since its inception and has grown, if anything, stronger during the intervening years. The modern jazz movement that emerged in the 1940s was especially important in crystallizing the nascent aesthetics of abundance that had been implicit in earlier jazz: this generation of musicians was creating not just another new sound but rather establishing that the sound of newness was now a permanent attribute of jazz music. With their numerous substitute chords, intricate melody lines, and jarring interludes, the beboppers were asserting that the repetitive formulas of earlier jazz were no longer applicable. As Gary Giddins has written: "They were in rebellion not only against the banalization of 'our' music by commercial interests, but against the morass of cliches that governed so many improvisations. What they offered was not simply an elevated harmonic intricacy, but a new articulation."[1]

In this regard modern jazz was quite unlike the primitive art forms to which black music is so often compared. Repeti-

tion, not original variation, is the most salient aspect of primitive art; such works attempt to achieve a "virtuous" boredom,
in which absence of variety serves as a positive attribute. As
anthropologist Edmund Leach, in his essay on primitive aesthetics, has remarked: "The forms of primitive art are original
only in the sense that they are alien to the European tradition; in their own context they are often in the highest degree
conventional and academic—originality is an admired virtue
among modern European artists; in most primitive contexts it
is a vice."[2] Especially in music, primitivism moves its audience
through a hypnotic repetition, not through the abundance of
its musical motives. Such repetitions have certainly made their
way into jazz, but only recently—the one-chord drones of
modal jazz would probably have scandalized Jelly Roll Morton or King Oliver.

It has long been tempting to view these first generations of
jazz performers as intuitive artists whose music succeeded
more through its emotional immediacy than through any intellectual content. Their music, in other words, is seen as similar to primitive art in its hypnotic, instinctive power; its intellectual component—its creativity and ceaseless variety—is,
from this perspective, a lesser or non-existent virtue. To the
extent that this view has been discarded—and it has only been
partially discarded—it too was largely the result of the modern
jazz movement. Not only did this new music change the way
many listeners viewed contemporary jazz artists, but it also
paved the way for serious consideration of an earlier generation of performers—men such as Duke Ellington, Don Redman, Bix Beiderbecke, Earl Hines, and others. Not that these
musicians had not been praised before, but they had been
lauded most often in ways that saw only one side of their contribution. For many of Ellington's earliest listeners, his band's
most salient characteristic was its "jungle sound" and its intoxicating rhythms. When we listen to the Ellington perfor-

mances of the 1930s and 1940s today, much different virtues stand out: innovations in song structure, arrangements, use of soloists, and the like. The music has not changed, but our perspective has. The modern jazz musician, by taking himself seriously as an artist, has validated the intellectual component of his music as well as added retrospective luster to the reputations of those who went before him.

In point of fact, jazz and especially modern jazz may be best viewed as the exact *opposite* of those schools of art—primitivism, minimalism, and others—which reduce the content of art. Modern jazz may well exemplify a sharply contrasting sensibility: it may offer the listener too much content, too much variety, too much flux and change. Frederick Turner, summarizing the research done by the Werner Reimers Stiftung study group on the biological foundation of aesthetics, has described precisely these two extremes:

> Much of our work has showed that experimental human subjects show a crude preference—which we had no choice but to regard as the raw material of aesthetic judgment—for perceptual experiences which met and fully engaged the sensitivities and capacities of the various senses. That is, they were neither so simple as to bore the nervous system, nor so complex as to overload it.[3]

Such research is of particular relevance to music, and serves to validate the similar conclusions of earlier writers on the subject, for example aesthetician Leonard Meyer, whose seminal book *Emotion and Meaning in Music* demonstrated how all music, from the humblest nursery song to the most ambitious opera, balanced these same two extremes.[4] On the one hand music uses repetition to create expectations on the part of the listener, but on the other hand it destroys these same expectations by employing false cadences, unexpected modulations, shifts in tone, and other similar devices. For Meyer, the binary opposition between the creation and frustration of expectation is at the root of our emotional reactions to music. From this perspective, music that has either too much or too little content is, put simply, *bad* music. It fails to engage its audience either by frustrating them through its incoherence or by boring them to tears.

Many contemporary works of art consciously err on the side of boredom—their creators aim for an exemplary purification which requires a narrowing of scope and a diminution of content. Such works may achieve, in the most extreme cases, what critic Roland Barthes refers to as the "degree zero" of style. Jazz during the modern period, in contrast, has come to represent something much different—it is music *packed* with content, it hums with constant activity. As such, it pushes the listener towards the limits of his ability to process and comprehend what he is hearing. Very few works of music—perhaps a Bach fugue or concerto—offer a melody line as complex as a bebop improvisation; and, like the Bach composition, the bebop solo has the potential to use this abundance and variety to good measure. At its best—for example in the justly celebrated Massey Hall recording of the mid-1950s, which captured Charlie Parker, Dizzy Gillespie, and Bud Powell playing at peak form—this kind of jazz can almost sweep the listener away with the momentum and seemingly endless creativity of its complex melodic statements. Yet this approach to music, by its very nature, also risks achieving another, less satisfying result. By overwhelming the listener with too much variety, it risks losing him entirely. Modern jazz, at its worst, creates another type of boredom, one in which the listener has ceased to care about the music and where it is going.

This gestalt quality of modern jazz has been reflected in an equally striking split among those who listen to and write about it. While most critics have been content to accept the music on its own terms, a smaller group—comprised mostly of jazz "outsiders" such as Philip Larkin and Henry Pleasants— have rebelled against precisely this institutionalized excess, as they see it, in most postwar jazz. Their response to the cease- less virtuosity of this music has been along the lines of Lar- kin's citation of Dr. Johnson: "Difficult, madam? Would it were impossible!" Polemics such as these, whether right or wrong, reflect the equivocal nature of the music itself. It is as though, with the advent of modern jazz, the contemporary improviser were handed a two-edged sword which, depending on how it were used, could either vitalize or vitiate his craft.

III

Seldom can such broad changes in an art form's underlying values be attributed to a single individual; yet the opposite approach—one which assigns innovations to "schools" of art- ists, movements, or simply to the "spirit of the times"—is per- haps even more flawed. More often than not, one individual paves the way for such transformations, whether motivated by pure inspiration, economic pressures, or mere boredom with existing conventions. Without this individual the world of art would certainly have gone on, but differently, less richly. Those who attribute such changes in art to "the spirit of beauty as it awakens to self-knowledge" (Hegel) or, more empirically, to "changes of climate, government, religion and language" (Hume) have forgotten the essential individual artist in studying the art.

In the case of modern jazz, such an individual was Charlie Parker. Certainly there were other individuals who made important contributions to the modern jazz movement—trum- peter Dizzy Gillespie, pianists Bud Powell and Thelonious Monk, guitarist Charlie Christian, drummers Kenny Clarke and Max Roach, to name only a few—but Parker's contribution was arguably the greatest of them all, and certainly the most pervasive. His influence on other musicians extended far beyond his own instrument, the alto saxophone, and eventually transformed the way all of the jazz instruments were played. Lennie Tristano, one of the most gifted pianists of the bebop period, exaggerated only slightly when he claimed: "If Charlie Parker wanted to invoke plagiarism laws, he could sue everybody who's made a record in the last ten years."[5]

Parker's life story has been recounted often and at length; even so, the story as commonly told has more the trappings of mythic legend than of contemporary biography. Kansas City, where he was born in August 1920, was a hotbed of political corruption and intense musical activity; the easy-swinging, blues-inflected jazz of Parker's youth—distinctive enough to be christened "Kansas City style"—featured some of the finest musicians jazz has ever produced. Artists in local residence, or frequently passing through, would have included Count Basie, Ben Webster, Mary Lou Williams, Andy Kirk, Jimmy Rushing, Herschel Evans, Buddy Tate, Jay McShann, and, Parker's greatest influence, Lester Young.

At first, however, Parker's inspiration came from none of these sources but from the radio broadcasts of Rudy Vallee; under the later undetectable influence of this unlikely musician, thirteen-year-old Charlie Parker convinced his mother to buy him an alto saxophone. After a brief preoccupation with the instrument, his interest diminished, and the alto was passed on to a friend. Later, during his early high school years Parker's interest in music reasserted itself and, after a brief period of study, he began playing in a local band with pianist Lawrence Keyes (who was nicknamed, almost inevitably it would seem, "Eighty-eight" Keyes). In this environment Parker matured quickly from a spoiled mama's boy—his father had left home when Charlie was nine and was stabbed to death during a quarrel several years later—to a far too worldly youth. By his mid-teens he was already married, a professional musician, and a drug user. Parker later remarked that he began dissipating at age twelve and using heroin at age fifteen; other sources, including his first wife Rebecca, insist that his narcotics problem developed a couple years later. In either case the habit started early in Parker's life and stayed with him for much of his all too short career. Parker was influential in this respect as well, and for a while more than a few fellow musicians emulated his unfortunate lifestyle almost as much as they did his music.

But it is as a musician that Parker most interests us. Yet despite time-honored stereotypes of youthful virtuosity, Parker's musical development during these years was, by all accounts, a gradual process. Bassist Gene Ramey later recalled Charlie as "the saddest thing in [Keyes] band." On at least two occasions Parker embarrassed himself at local jam sessions: at one of these Parker was playing with members of the Count Basie band when he got caught up in the racing double-time tempo; Basie's drummer Jo Jones rendered his negative judgment on the young alto player's performance by lifting a cymbal off its stand and sending it flying through the air to crash at Parker's feet. Such anecdotes, whether exaggerated or not, do not exactly bespeak early developing genius.

Soon after, in the summer of 1937, Parker joined the band of George Lee, which had been engaged to play at a resort spot in the Ozarks. During this period he studied harmony with the band's guitarist and listened assiduously to a stack of Count Basie albums he had brought with him. From these he learned the tenor solos of Lester Young, Basie's star saxophonist, note for note. Further refinements were no doubt made during Parker's ensuing apprenticeship with saxophonist Buster Smith, whose mastery of double-time playing had a profound influence on the young altoist.

Smith left for New York in 1938, intending to send for the rest of the band if he found work. After several months Parker followed, heading first to Chicago where alto saxophonist Goon Gardner was sufficiently impressed with his playing to provide him with a clarinet and get him some work. By this time Parker had clearly developed much of his extraordinary technique on the saxophone; but perhaps more striking than his mature if unfocused mastery of the horn was his bedraggled appearance—singer Billy Eckstine remembered Parker from this period as "the raggedest guy you'd want to see."

Several weeks after he arrived in Chicago, Parker had pawned his clarinet and was on his way to New York. Once arrived he found his mentor Smith, who put him up while he looked for some way of earning a living in the Big Apple. At one point during this period Parker was working as a dishwasher at Jimmy's Chicken Shack, a Harlem nightspot which occasionally featured the great blind jazz pianist Art Tatum. Despite his non-union status Parker managed to find a few musical gigs, most of them fairly informal. More important were the final steps in Parker's musical education which took place at this time. In a later interview, he recalled what seemed to him to be the crucial breakthrough in his playing:

> I remember one night before Monroe's I was jamming in a chili house on Seventh Avenue between 139th and 140th. It was December 1939. Now I'd been getting bored with the stereotyped changes that were being used at the time, and I kept thinking there's bound to be something else. I could hear it sometimes but I couldn't play it. Well, that night I was working over "Cherokee," and

as I did I found that by using the higher intervals of a chord as a melody line and backing them with appropriately related changes, I could play the thing I'd been hearing. I came alive.[6]

Parker's "boredom" with the stereotyped changes would eventually lead to a revolution in jazz the likes of which have not been seen since. Shortly after, Parker rejoined Jay McShann, and the few recordings of the band made during this period document his virtuosity and his almost unique conception of jazz improvisation. No recordings exist from his ensuing work with the Earl Hines band, but this ensemble likely served as a finishing school for him as well as for a group of like-minded modernists, most notably trumpeter Dizzy Gillespie. Parker's affiliation with Hines was short-lived; soon he was recording as a leader for the Savoy label, and his reputation was no longer generated mainly by word-of-mouth but by an increasing number of widely available recordings.

Modern jazz was no longer under wraps. Gillespie's flair for publicity combined with the obvious newness of the music to create a public awareness that extended beyond the jazz world. Bebop, however, was not destined to be popular music—certainly not like big band music: the melodic lines were too complex; the time signature was invariably 4/4, but the rhythmic placement was so subtle that more than a few listeners had trouble finding the downbeat; the fast numbers were faster than anyone had played jazz before, while the occasional slow number might be played at a snail's pace. The typical trappings of popular jazz—vocals, catchy arrangements, dance tunes—were largely absent. This was music that aimed primarily at communicating the musicians' creative prowess and only secondarily at pleasing the audience.

Nonetheless, the public mystique of bebop was sufficient to warrant a trip to the West Coast for Parker and Gillespie in late 1945. Although a contingent of California musicians were already devotees of the music, the overall response to the group's engagement at Billy Berg's in Los Angeles was lukewarm at best. The band's visit out West was short-lived, but Parker stayed on; whether due to drug problems or to tardiness pure and simple, Parker missed the flight home just as he had missed several performances.

Narcotics were, however, a factor when Parker's July 1946 record session with the Dial label foundered. His first session with Dial in March had been remarkable—his renditions of "Yardbird Suite," "Moose the Mooche," "Ornithology," and "Night in Tunisia" were extraordinary; his playing, especially on the latter number's four-bar break, displayed a technical virtuosity and rhythmic sophistication as great as any musician in jazz has done since. But the July follow-up session found Parker barely able to stand and his playing slurred and uneven. Later that evening he twice wandered naked into the lobby of his hotel; after returning to his room, he apparently fell asleep while smoking and set off a fire, which brought firefighters and policemen to his door. Parker was arrested, served ten days in jail, and then was transferred to the Camarillo State Hospital for a six-month stay. After his release, largely due to the efforts of his record producer and eventual biographer Ross Russell, Parker decided that he had had enough of California. Soon he was back in New York.

The Camarillo experience perhaps served only to enhance the Parker mystique, and from that point on he was as much a legend as a musician. His ensuing recordings, mostly done for producer Norman Granz, saw Parker playing with string orchestras, vocal ensembles, in jam sessions, and in all-star bands—in short, he was now the accepted master with a commercial audience that demanded novelty and which guaranteed that any record he made would be bought, any performance he gave would be attended.

Parker's recordings during the 1950s, especially his studio dates, reflect an easy mastery and relaxed virtuosity that may not possess the sense of experimentation and intensity of his earlier works but are exceptional products nonetheless. His day-to-day life, however, was anything but relaxed, and the anecdotes and legends about Parker's "eccentricities" grew proportional to his fame. Lives such as his take their toll: at his death in 1955 the attending physician estimated his age at fifty-three. In fact he was only thirty-four.

Parker's contributions to jazz far exceeded the sum of his own recordings and performances. His style and sound—his very conception of jazz—became a standard for other musicians. The technical requirements for jazz playing increased significantly due to the influence of Parker and his colleagues in the modern jazz movement. But even more compelling was the modernists' attitude towards innovation: their quest for new and interesting sounds; their willingness to experiment; their sense of themselves as creative artists and not mere entertainers. These represented a powerful inoculation against popular art's inherent tendency to substitute boring formulas for creativity, to accept repetition of past successes as the model for future behavior.

IV

Broadly speaking, there are two opposed aesthetic attitudes towards boring art. The first view, the "Andy Warhol" approach, sees boredom as a virtue. As odd as this may seem to the average person, more than a few artists have subscribed to this view, at least implicitly: minimalist composers such as Steve Reich and Philip Glass; contemporary writers such as Raymond Carver and Ann Beattie; filmmakers such as Warhol; painters such as Rothko or Mondrian. Warhol's film *Sleep*—an eight-hour film of a person sleeping—is a classic example of this approach carried to an extreme. Carver's short stories are closer to the mainstream, and more commercial, but they betray the same underlying approach. With such artists, lack of variety is not a flaw but, rather, an essential part of their work.

The opposing view, one which sees boredom as a vice and aims at an intellectually and emotionally absorbing art, is at the heart of the modern jazz tradition which developed out of Charlie Parker. Parker's legacy was a virtuosity which delighted in the variety and complexity of its musical expressions, at the sheer abundance of what it could create. Such self-conscious virtuosity was once compatible with modernism in other arts—witness, for example, the elaborate prose of a Proust or the wide-ranging musical palette of a Stravinsky—but apparently no longer. What we call "post-modernism" (for want of a better name) finds such exhibitions of technique to be in bad taste, and any quest for "excessive" variety in art to be somewhat suspect. The high status accorded to minimalist approaches to art is the most obvious example of this change in temperament, but by no means the only one.

Jazz has often paid surprisingly little attention to what passes as fashionable in other arts, and over the years this has been one of its saving graces. But this isolation from the changing currents of cultural fashion is diminishing with time; schools of art which one would think were, almost by necessity, alien to jazz are beginning to exert an influence on it. "New Age" jazz, minimalist jazz, and much of what passes for fusion or modal jazz are nurtured on repetition and monotony, much like the other contemporary arts that seek a "virtuous" boredom. These seem to be more reactions against the jazz tradition rather than extensions of it. So much so that many have vehemently argued that, for example, "New Age" music is not jazz at all, but a different type of improvised music. Certainly this argument has been used often enough, and wrongly, in the past—Charlie Parker's music was not jazz according to many swing era musicians, just as Ornette Coleman's music was not jazz according to many be-boppers. In retrospect, these latter styles seem part of a nat-ural evolution: the transition from Louis Armstrong to Les-ter Young to Charlie Parker to Ornette Coleman makes sense as the development of a single tradition. In contrast, the "New Age" music of the Windham Hill label or minimalist jazz, such as Anthony Davis's assimilations of Balinese game-lan music, are different things entirely. They are almost negations of the jazz tradition: the abundance, the variety, the creativity of the jazz tradition—what critic Whitney Bal-liett rightly calls the "sound of surprise"—are largely lacking in them.

At the other extreme are those descendants of the modern jazz tradition who, by taking the dictates of variety and free-dom to their limits, offer an incoherent, unlistenable product. Unlike the other group, these are true children of the jazz heritage and the roots of their music can be traced back to jazz's earliest performers. Yet such a lineage does not make this music any less threatening to the tradition that gave it birth. In an odd sort of way, this music ultimately achieves a different sort of boredom. One that is more enriched by the tradition, but far less artistic or vital than that tradition.

V

How refreshing it would be if the jazz critic—as well as those in other "high" arts—were to follow the lead of the common man, who may not know what art is but does know what is boring. Precedents for such a dramatic change are no doubt quite rare: serious thinkers on art from Socra-tes to Susan Sontag have usually emphasized less mundane elements of art; most have preferred to treat a work's virtues and flaws as though they were inherent in the work itself, rather than stemming from a *relationship* between the artistic product and its viewer. The layman takes the exact opposite approach to art; hence his aesthetic vocabulary is laden with relationship words: terms such as "entertaining," "interesting," and "annoying," which focuses on his own reactions to the work in question. Professional aestheticians adopt a far different vocabulary; they speak of "form," "symmetry," "beauty," "sublimity," and so on, in a manner which often suggests that these qualities have an independent existence unrelated to a work's audience. For philosophers, as for many artists, the existence of an independent and intelligent audience, with its own critical faculties, is much to be lamented. Such pedestrian associations, they seem to say, only serve to taint the pristine beauty of art. Their reverence for the work of art makes it into a thing apart, like a saint's relic, which is not to be comprehended in human terms.

The inability, or unwillingness, of most modern critics to talk about boredom perhaps reveals a deep-rooted insecurity. A critic's admission of boredom always holds open the possible retort that he, and not the work of art, is at fault. If the critic were more aware, sensitive, intelligent, he would have seen the work in all its splendor and beauty. Art critic John Perreault, in his defense of minimalism, articulates precisely this point:

> A great deal of the boredom associated with Minimal Art is in the mind of the beholder. The viewer will be bored if he does not know what to look for or if he expects something that is not there.[7]

Given the prevalence of such views, it is far safer for the critics to avoid any reference to his relationship to the work of art; he risks the least by talking in the most abstract and even meaningless terms about the "work in itself." About feelings, the less said the better. But the "work in itself," like Kant's thing-in-itself, is a metaphysical notion which adds nothing to our comprehension of the work in question. Are not works of art important because of the impact they have on us? And are not some works interesting or entertaining, while others are insufferably boring? We all know these things to be true, yet—strange to say—such simple facts rarely inform our critical judgments.

Jazz, more than the other arts, stands to gain the most from such a recognition of basic aesthetic values. Its evolution from a popular art to a serious art has probably been, on the whole, a positive development; yet this change has been accompanied by undeniable problems. The relationship of audience to artist in the popular arts is, for the most part, quite unambiguous: the audience expects to be *engaged* by the work of art; works that fail to achieve this do not survive—if only because they soon have no audience. This kind of relationship is far from perfect—it no doubt suffers from the vagaries of popular fashion and the limitations (such as in sophistication and understanding) of the mass audience—but in its own way it is an honest relationship. It makes no pretenses. The high arts, for all their greater sophistication, often lack this honesty in their critical appraisals; snobbishness, scholasticism, ideologies of various sorts, elitism, academic considerations—these and other forms of inauthenticity are much more likely to cloud the critical capacity. As it gains in credibility, jazz risks falling prey to these assorted ways of obfuscating the essential relationship between jazz artist and jazz audience. The end result is a complete flip-flop of traditional values—music that is engaging or entertaining is seen not just as possessing *lesser* virtues but actually becomes suspect in some undefined way.

Roland Barthes has written eloquently of the "pleasures of

the text," and his call for an erotics of aesthetic judgement has been a resonant theme in much recent critical literature. But why stop with pleasure? The pursuit of pleasure can only exist side by side with the ever present chance of boredom and erotic frustration. The banishment of boredom transforms Barthes's erotics into mere aesthetic onanism. The right to declare one's boredom, and to take steps to relieve it—these are not just the critic's prerogatives but, in fact, his responsibilities. Let us not neglect the pleasures of the text, but neither let us forget the pleasures of not finishing the text, of leaving the museum or jazz club, of not renewing the subscription to the symphony. Such acts of outraged boredom may have just as much aesthetic validity as do the most serious meditations on the highest ideals of symmetry and formal beauty.

VII

Jazz as Song

> We were all tired and everybody was sort of
> asleep on the bus. Pres was sitting in an aisle
> seat, dozing, when [a well-known saxophonist]
> took out his horn and began walking up and
> down playing his licks. Nobody paid any atten-
> tion to him, so finally he went over to Lester
> and said, "Hey, Pres, whadda ya think of that?"
> Pres, his eyes half closed, said, "Yes, Lady—, but
> can you sing me a song?"
>
> STAN GETZ
> *Downbeat,* May 19, 1966

I

We should perhaps be thankful for second-rate art. The poor-
est practitioners of any craft are often, like clumsy magicians
or awkward liars, more revealing than their betters. Even more
than the masterpiece, the worst art serves as a crucible in
which a period's superficial veneer is melted away to reveal
the bald assumptions, the prevalent ideologies, the crassest
commonplaces of the times. Shakespeare is universal; it is
with a Thomas Kyd or a Cyril Tourneur that we encounter a
true Elizabethan.

At its worst, the work of the second-rate or neophyte artist
collapses into a painful, if unintentional parody which magni-
fies the flaws of a whole generation. Once well-versed in the
art of the second rate, the critic can return to the masterpiece

with an acute ability to perceive the artist's blind spots and pitfalls—lapses which otherwise remain in relief.

Mediocrity can no doubt be found in any art form, but its presence is perhaps especially acute in the world of jazz. With its extreme emphasis on improvisation, jazz lacks the external polish and precision which can compensate for lapses in more leisurely constructed arts. The jazz artist is expected to produce a new and different performance each and every night; any rote display of a solo he has prepared in advance not only receives the scorn of musicians and critics but actually seems to run counter to the spirit of the music. The limitations of spontaneous creation are no doubt real, but they have become part and parcel of jazz music—as soon as the jazz instrumentalist begins to plan his solos in advance, he ceases, by that very act, to be a *jazz* soloist and becomes a type of composer; as such, he must be evaluated in an entirely different context and with entirely different standards.

This social context for jazz has radically shaped the way the jazz musician views his craft. Unlike artists in other fields, he becomes ludicrous if he appears to wait for moments of enlightened inspiration before beginning to create. The stereotyped image of the artist awaiting his muse may fit, more or less, with the actual practice of the sculptor, the novelist, the painter, or even the composer of serious music, but it bears little relation to the realities of the jazz performance. The world of classical music, for example, can point to a figure such as Hugo Wolf as exemplifying this familiar artistic image: from February 1888 through June 1890 Wolf composed with feverish intensity, producing some 174 songs including many of his greatest masterpieces; in contrast, from 1892 to 1894 he was able to compose virtually no viable music. Wolf's alternation between inspired composition and periods of barrenness, whatever might have been the underlying physical cause, fits well with our received notions of artistic production. Art, it is commonly believed, is not a commodity which can be produced with assembly-line efficiency. It comes, good or bad, on its own terms or not at all.

What are we to make, in this light, of the jazz musician, who walks on stage by appointment, without a prepared score and with little clear idea of how his improvisations will develop that evening? He creates *de novo* again and again, night after night, and is evaluated in the context of this constant musical activity. Even the recording situation, treated by classical artists such as Glenn Gould or Vladimir Horowitz with scrupulous care (as an unnamed recording engineer once joked: "Today we record the left hand, tomorrow we'll start on the right"), is typically treated by jazz performers with the same casual attitude characteristic of their live performances. Most of the jazz idiom's greatest recorded masterpieces—the King Oliver Creole Band recordings in the 1920s; the Charlie Parker Dial sessions in the 1940s; the classic Blue Note albums in the 1960s and the many fine ECM recordings in the 1980s—were done with very little studio time and even little or no rehearsal time. In contrast, more carefully planned jazz events—for example the attempts to pair Charlie Parker with prepared arrangements for string orchestra—have worn poorly with time and often seem to lack the vitality so essential to jazz.

This reliance on spontaneity brings with it many hidden costs. If the jazz artist is not permitted to wait for moments of inspiration, is it any wonder that so many jazz performances seem uninspired? If the jazz artist is expected to create music, time and time again, in noisy and often inhospitable settings, is it any wonder that he frequently just goes through the motions? Indeed, the measure of mediocrity found in any art form could hardly find a more fertile ground for growth than in the hectic and thoughtless world of jazz. It is an art which, by its culture as well as its social context and conditions, must struggle for most of the comforts which the other arts presuppose.

The unrelenting emphasis on impromptu creation often forces the jazz artist to rely continually on stock effects and set patterns. With a memorized vocabulary of hot licks, the soloist will never be caught without something to say. Yet, in the most extreme instance, these effects can come to dominate the musician's work. So much so that the freshness and spontaneity which is integral to jazz may only *appear* to be present. In fact, the performance becomes a pastiche of cliches, patterns, and licks.

In his seminal work on Homer and oral narrative, *The Singer of Tales,* Albert Lord points out that improvisational verse brings with it the same reliance on stock formulas. "Under the pressure of rapid composition in performance," the aspiring singer of tales soon learns set patterns which fit commonly used metrical forms:

> . . . his training is preeminently one of learning to produce lines. Part of the process is accomplished by remembering and using phrases heard from other singers. This constitutes one element in the continuity of oral epic style. The phrases help to establish in the singer's experience a series of patterns. . . . At the same time, by necessity, because he does not remember all the phrases which he needs, he is forced at the moment of his private performances *to form phrases on the basis of the patterns.*[1] (emphasis mine)

The great improvisational artist—whether in oral poetry or jazz music or whatever art form—transcends these limitations of spontaneous creation. The repeated tags applied to characters in Homer can hardly be said to detract from the grandeur of the *Odyssey;* nor do the set chromatic patterns that reappear throughout Charlie Parker's work mar the beauty of his improvisations. In these works the set phrase is integrated into a whole which is much more than a collection of such phrases. Even the patterns themselves can be the occasion for a fresh creation; for example, a chromatic phrase which Parker uses in bar 64 of his recording of "She Rote" reappears against different harmonies in "Blues (Fast)" and is set against a different place in the bar in "Bloomdido"; again it can be heard with a slight variation and a still different rhythmic placement in his recording of "Merry-Go-Round." One could cite many other examples; it suffices to point out that, although this was a phrase that Parker had "under his fingers," his use of it was always musical. The freshness with which he employed it made it more than just a memorized lick.

These same phrases, which in the hands of a Charlie Parker were used with immense creativity and originality, often seemed hackneyed and uninspired with their rote repetition by Parker's more facile disciples. Shortly after Parker's death, bassist Charles Mingus remarked with sarcasm that the other jazz musicians would be at a loss now that they no longer had Parker to imitate: "Most of the soloists at Birdland had to wait for Parker's next record in order to find out what to play. What will they do now?"[2] Jazz, by its very nature, encourages such excesses of imitation. In the visual arts, by comparison, movements such as cubism, abstract expressionism, pop art, and the like may have engendered imitators, but the basic premise of such developments was that individual expression was more important than superficial technical fluency. The manifestos which have characterized most twentieth-century art—spawning schools of surrealists, imagists, vorticists, and so on—have been notably absent in jazz. The prevailing belief that jazz is an instinctive rather than deliberative art has made such clear definitions of stylistic intent seem out of place in the jazz world. The end result has been that most modern jazz, like pre-modern art in other areas, still exhibits a fascination with superficial virtuosity; it displays the most extreme reverence for technical fluency and encourages the repetition of the established vocabulary of past masters. By its unrelenting emphasis on spontaneity it has become, ironically, anything but spontaneous.

II

It has become commonplace to say of the best jazz singers that they "use their voices like instruments." In fact, the opposite is much more true: the great jazz musician aspires to using his instrument like a voice. He aspires to that unmediated connection between the conception and the expression of a musical idea which is so characteristic of the human voice. The best jazz musicians, regardless of their instrument, *are* singers.

To describe the successful jazz musician in these terms is to do more than apply a colorful, if somewhat vague, metaphor. The essentially vocal tones employed by the first generation of jazz instrumentalists—the inflected notes, the slurs, the moans, the growls, the glides—were perhaps the most striking elements of the new music. The much imitated cornet solo by King Oliver on his early recording of "Dippermouth Blues," to cite but one example, derived its power *not* from the notes Oliver played—indeed, when notated, the solo seems positively monotonous, with its endless repetition of a couple of simple phrases—but from the evocative vocal tone that Oliver imparted to his notes. Jazz scholars know very little about how King Oliver viewed his craft, but at least one noteworthy statement has come down to us: Oliver is on record as saying that it took him ten years to develop his *tone* on the cornet. It was precisely this emphasis on creating an individual tone, an almost vocal tone, that made Oliver's music, like that of his contemporary Sidney Bechet or his protégé Louis Armstrong, so strikingly different from notated instrumental music. Such music possessed a warmth and human sound previously found only in vocal music. Armstrong's later work made this relationship even clearer: the striking similarity between Armstrong the trumpeter and Armstrong the singer could not be denied. So much so that one could imagine a listener, familiar only with Armstrong's trumpet work, recognizing his style in a vocal piece, or vice versa.

The best jazz musicians of later generations have also shared this same distinction. Coleman Hawkins, Lester Young, Charlie Parker, Thelonious Monk, Miles Davis, Stan Getz, John Coltrane, Bill Evans, Ornette Coleman—each of these justly celebrated improvisers demonstrated a concern, almost a fastidious concern, with the quality and individuality of his sound. Even when playing a simple written passage—or perhaps just one or two notes—their musical identity comes across clearly and immediately. Miles Davis need only play a C scale, and no jazz listener could confuse him with any other trumpeter.

But saying that the best jazz musicians are "singers of songs" implies even more than the presence of this vocal quality in their playing. It also suggests that their improvisations are more than collections of "hip" phrases and crowd-rousing clichés; instead they possess the musical coherence that one expects in a song. They exhibit a sense of balance and proportion and an emotional integrity that makes them true musical statements. In the context of a song, musical virtuosity exists only as a means of expression and not as an end in itself. Similarly, the rhythmic drive of a song is not a purely mechanical sense of momentum but is part of the music, enhancing it and helping to develop it. These aesthetic considerations, no less than issues of musical technique, inform the playing of jazz's greatest musicians. Perhaps no other jazz artist ex-

emplified these virtues more clearly than the legendary saxophonist Lester Young. His work, more than that of any other
jazz musician, achieved the musicality of song.

III

Early jazz, like feudal society, had its own lines of aristocracy.
Count Basie, Duke Ellington, King Oliver, King Bolden: figures such as these constituted jazz's nobility, and their patri-
archal bearing and equanimity were all the more remarkable
when one considers the many barriers society placed against
black artists in their day.

Democratic institutions may lack the charm of old world
monarchies, but in at least one instance they made their mark.
Lester Young, the diffident tenor saxophonist who sprang to
fame with the Basie band came to be known as "Prez" (short
for President), and his strikingly individualistic playing inspired an almost patriotic fervor among his fans and disciples.
(Indeed one well-known musician modeled his style so closely
on Young's, that he was immediately tagged the "Vice-Prez.")

Billie Holiday, in her autobiography *Lady Sings the Blues*,
recalls how she gave Young his nickname:

> When it came to a name for Lester, I always felt he was
> the greatest, so his name had to be the greatest. In this
> country kings or counts or dukes don't amount to noth-
> ing. The greatest man around then was Franklin D. Roo-
> sevelt. So I started calling him the President. It got
> shortened to Prez, but it still means what it was meant to
> mean—the top man in this country.[3]

Few artists have ever emerged on the jazz scene with their
style so fully formed. Young's first recorded solo, on the Basie
band's "Shoe Shine Boy," made on October 4, 1936, is considered by many to be his finest. Yet, despite his early matu-

rity, Young's term of presidency was to last only through two brief administrations. With his induction into the army in September 1944, Young's most creative musical period came to an end.

Young's tenure with the army was ill-fated almost from the start. Three months into military service he injured himself during an obstacle course exercise. While hospitalized he was diagnosed as being in a "constitutional psychopathic state manifested by drug addiction (marijuana, barbiturates), chronic alcoholism, and nomadism." Shortly after, on February 1, Young was arrested for possession of drugs. He was court-martialed, given a dishonorable discharge, and forced to serve ten months at army disciplinary barracks in Georgia.

The transcripts of Young's court martial, uncovered by research in 1980, cast a penetrating light on the prevalence of drugs among musicians of that period:

Q. You are a musician by profession?
A. Yes, sir.
Q. Had you played in a band or orchestra in California?
A. Count Basie. I played with him for ten years.
Q. Had you been taking narcotics for some time?
A. For ten years. This is my 11th year.
Q. When did you start taking them?
A. Well, sir, playing in the band we would play a lot of one nighters. I would stay up and play another dance and leave and that is the only way I could keep up.
Q. Any other . . . musicians take them?
A. Yes, all that I know.[4]

Young was financially secure during the postwar years. Consistently placing towards the top in polls conducted by *Downbeat, Metronome,* and *Esquire,* Young was able to command a salary of $1,000 a week while on tour as part of Norman Granz's "Jazz at the Philharmonic" entourage, and his annual income, during this period, was as high as $50,000.[5] Commercial and critical success, however, seemed to have little effect in healing the psychological scars left by Young's army experience. Taciturn by nature, he became even more introverted after the war. His playing, despite the critical accolades, was also affected. Like Bud Powell, that other tormented genius of jazz's transitional years, Young at his best could approach his earlier achievements, but would never surpass them.

Yet this does Prez no disservice. Few artists will ever match the sculpted beauty of his early work. John Hammond, whose ability to recognize talent is almost legendary—his discoveries include Billie Holiday, Count Basie, Benny Goodman, Bob Dylan, and Bruce Springsteen—echoed the sentiments of many when he wrote in *Downbeat* in February 1937 that Young was "without a doubt the greatest tenor player in the country . . . the most original and inventive saxophonist I have ever heard."[6] Even on his first recordings one could hear the striking elements that set Young apart from virtually every other saxophonist of his generation.

At that time Coleman Hawkins was the undisputed master of the tenor saxophone—indeed, contemporary musicians can scarcely imagine the dominating influence Hawkins had over the way the saxophone was played in jazz. Yet Young's style was the antithesis of Hawkins's playing in almost every respect: Hawkins's tone was thick and expansive, Young's was light and airy; Hawkins's approach was admired for its harmonic inventivenes, Young's approach was primarily melodic; Hawkins used a strongly pronounced vibrato, Young used almost none; Hawkins's playing strongly accented the rhythmic pulse, Lester floated over the beats.

In essence, Lester's sound was the sound of modernism in jazz. Today the music of Coleman Hawkins, for all its undeniable virtues, definitely sounds as though it were from a by-gone era. Young's solos, in contrast, sound newly minted. At the time of his professional debut, however, Young was anything but admired for his distinctive approach to the music. In 1934 he replaced Hawkins in Fletcher Henderson's band, only to find himself in a hostile environment. Lester later recalled:

> The whole band was buzzing on me, because I had taken Hawk's place. I didn't have the same kind of sound he had. I was rooming at the Henderson's house, and Leora Henderson would wake me early in the morning and play Hawkins' records for me so I could play like he did.[7]

Several months later, Young left Henderson to rejoin the Count Basie band. It was during this period that Young produced those classic recordings which were to have a powerful and lasting impact on the development of jazz. In particular, his small group collaborations with Billie Holiday stand out as quintessential examples of that rich hybrid born from a union of instrumental jazz and the American popular song.

The beauty of the music, though, was often at odds with the inner strife of the musician. Even before the war, negative experiences such as those Young faced during his tenure with Henderson led him to put up many psychological barriers against the outside world. Young, by all accounts, was a difficult person to get to know. His way with language was every bit as iconoclastic as his saxophone playing, and his scattered comments often required the interpretation of those skilled in "Lestertalk." "I feel a draft" was a typically enigmatic Young reference to any example, subtle or otherwise, of racism. Other musicians he would refer to as "Lady," and if they were in his band he might invite them to take another chorus with an off-hand "Have another helping"; at other times he might admonish them: "You've got to save your pennies to play with Prez"—which in translation simply meant that Lester was not planning on paying his group very well.

The army experiences only accentuated a form of psychological isolation that was already apparent from the start. Even in the midst of the affectionate accolades of fans, Young was distant and withdrawn, and even his successes turned around to haunt him: imitators would play his style almost as well as he could. The once distinctive stylist was reduced to lamenting, listening on the bandstand to a colleague: "I don't know whether to play like me or like Lady—, because he's playing so much like me."[8] In the end he felt that there was nothing of his own left for him to play.

Young's complaints, though heartfelt, were unfair to himself. Like other truly great innovators in jazz, his accomplishments stand above even the most careful imitations. His ability to communicate, to combine the passion of self-expression with the beauty achieved only through self-restraint, to give the saxophone a sound almost as natural and resonant as the human voice: these are achievements that ultimately distinguish Lester's work and assure it a secure and special place in the history of jazz.

Towards the end of his life those who visited Prez were often surprised to find him listening almost entirely to recordings of vocal music by pop singers such as Jo Stafford, Dick Haymes, and Frank Sinatra. Yet those who listened to the singing quality of his music could hardly find such a trait out of character. Billie Holiday summed it up best when she said of him: "Lester sings with his horn. You listen to him and you can almost hear the words."[9]

IV

The American popular song and jazz music, each developing from its own unique and distinct nineteenth-century predecessors, have maintained a symbiotic relationship during most of the twentieth century. While the two traditions have remained distinct, they have come to inspire each other, and much commerce has taken place over the years, and even today, between the two disciplines. The jazz instrumentalist still draws upon a repertoire of music created largely by composers such as Jerome Kern, George Gershwin, Richard Rodgers, Harold Arlen, Cole Porter, and Irving Berlin; just as singers of popular songs still rely upon a whole range of musical effects borrowed from jazz music.

The interaction between these two disciplines can be traced at least as far back as the 1920s when Bing Crosby, in the words of jazz critic Whitney Balliett, "almost by himself invented American popular singing."[10] Before Crosby, American singing lacked a unified tradition, relying upon the disparate achievements of minstrels, light classical singers, Irish tenors, folk singers, and the like. Crosby's much different and wholly original style evolved "in large part by listening to jazz musicians."[11] He studied the music of Armstrong and Ellington, later making records with both, and performed frequently with cornetist Bix Beiderbecke. Bix in particular, then largely unknown among the general public, left his mark on Crosby's singing. The phrasing, tonal quality, and rhythmic feel which Bing brought into his singing were thus not an outgrowth of an earlier American vocal tradition but rather a carryover from the essentially vocal quality of instrumental jazz in the 1920s.

Later singers of the American tradition continued to draw inspiration from jazz instrumentalists, and many—for example, Fats Waller, Nat Cole, Chet Baker, Billy Eckstine, and Mel Torme, to mention just a few—were jazz instrumentalists in their own right. The big band era was a fertile environment for such singers, as was, to a lesser extent, the later studio environment, with its large assortment of arrangers and musicians drawn from the jazz world. Popular singers such as Frank Sinatra and Tony Bennett may not be considered by the public as "jazz singers"—and this is probably quite fortunate for their financial well-being—but their work is unmistakably a part of the jazz tradition, and would be inconceivable without the contributions of that tradition.

This influence, however, worked the other way as well, if in a less visible manner. Jazz music has frequently benefited from the inspiration of song and of popular singers. Lester Young, the consummate singer on the tenor saxophone, often mentioned that he wanted to know the lyric of a song before he played it. Dexter Gordon, another tenor saxophonist, would preface his performance of a ballad with a brief recitation of part of the song's lyric. Figures as different as Jelly Roll Morton and Cecil Taylor have emphasized the singing of musical motifs in learning their music. These musicians saw themselves as performing songs—not études or technical exercises. These are jazz's "singers of songs."

Whether drawing from the traditional jazz repertoire—as with Dexter, Louis, or Lester—or singing songs marked by their own unique vision—as with Cecil Taylor or his contemporary Ornette Coleman—such musicians have provided the constant driving force that has elevated jazz from a folk art limited in geography and influence to an art form studied and emulated around the world. These singers of songs have viewed self-expression as a necessity and not merely as an option; for them jazz is the medium which allows the purest expression of feelings and attitudes uniquely their own. They are singers whose songs rise up in joy, in anger, in love, and in despair.

Notes

I. Louis Armstrong and Furniture Music

1. Nat Shapiro and Nat Hentoff, *Hear Me Talkin' to Ya'* (New York: Rinehart, 1955), 203.
2. Marshall Stearns, *The Story of Jazz* (New York: Oxford Univ. Press, 1956), 170.
3. Richard Hadlock, *Jazz Masters of the Twenties* (New York: Macmillan, 1965), 18.
4. Ezra Pound, *ABC of Reading* (London: Faber & Faber, 1951), 14.
5. Gunther Schuller, *Early Jazz* (New York: Oxford Univ. Press, 1968), 91.
6. Erik Satie, *Ecrits* (Paris: Champ Libre, 1977), 190.
7. *Ibid.*
8. Jose Ortega y Gasset, *The Dehumanization of Art,* trans., Helene Weyl (Princeton: Princeton Univ. Press, 1948), 14.
9. *Ibid.,* 26.
10. *Ibid.,* 29.
11. Quoted in Edgar Wind's *Art and Anarchy* (New York: Alfred A. Knopf, 1965), 71.
12. T. E. Hulme, *Speculations: Essays on Humanism and the Philosophy of Art,* ed., Herbert Read (London: Routledge & Kegan Paul, 1924), 122.
13. *Ibid.,* 104.
14. *Ibid.,* 97.

II. Jazz and the Primitivist Myth

1. Hugues Panassie, *Louis Armstrong* (New York: Scribner, 1971), 23–24.
2. *Ibid.*, 24.
3. Cited in Hoxie Neale Fairchild's *The Noble Savage: A Study in Romantic Naturalism* (New York: Columbia Univ. Press, 1928), 108–9.
4. *Ibid.*, 104–12.
5. This and following from Chris Goddard's *Jazz Away From Home* (New York: Paddington Press, 1979), 12–14.
6. Sidney Bechet, *Treat It Gentle* (New York: Hill and Wang, 1960), 128.
7. Leonard Feather, *The Encyclopedia of Jazz* (New York: Horizon Press, 1955), 101.
8. See James Lincoln Collier, "The Faking of Jazz," *The New Republic,* Nov. 18, 1985, pp. 33–40; see also follow-up correspondence in Dec. 16, 1985 issue, p. 6.
9. John Tasker Howard, *Our American Music* (New York: Thomas Cromwell, 1931).
10. Robert Delaunay, *Light and Color* (New York: Harry N. Abrams, Inc., 1967), 24.
11. Translated by Susan Suleiman in *Apollinaire on Art* (New York: Viking, 1972), 470–71.
12. Hugues Panassie, *The Real Jazz* (New York: Smith and Durrel, 1942), 6.
13. *Ibid.*
14. Robert Goffin, *Jazz: From the Congo to the Metropolitan* (New York: Doubleday, 1944), 167.
15. *Ibid.,* 124.
16. Bill Cole, *John Coltrane* (New York: Scribner, 1976), 6.
17. Winthrop Sargeant, *Jazz, Hot and Hybrid* (New York: Da Capo Press, 1975), 81.
18. Panassie, *The Real Jazz,* 7.
19. Pops Foster, *Pops Foster: The Autobiography of a New Orleans Jazzman* (Berkeley: Univ. of California Press, 1971), 43.

20. Rudi Blesh, *Shining Trumpets* (New York: Alfred A. Knopf, 1958), 160.
21. Foster, *The Autobiography of a New Orleans Jazzman*, 50.
22. Louis Armstrong, *Satchmo* (New York: Signet, 1955), 140–41.
23. James Lincoln Collier, *The Making of Jazz* (New York: Delta, 1978), 463.
24. Quoted in A. B. Spellman's *Black Music: Four Lives* (New York: Schocken Books, 1970), 84.
25. *Ibid.,* 90–91.
26. Cited in Leroy Ostransky's *Understanding Jazz* (New Jersey: Prentice-Hall, 1977), 244.
27. *Ibid.,* 246.
28. Spellman, *Black Music: Four Lives,* 80.
29. Recalled by Tynan in "Ornette: The First Beginning," *Downbeat,* July 21, 1960.
30. Published in *Downbeat,* July 1983, pp. 54–55.
31. This and below from Gary Giddins's excellent essay "Harmolodic Hoedown" from *Rhythm-a-ning* (New York: Oxford Univ. Press, 1985), 235–49.
32. Arthur C. Danto, *The State of the Art* (New York: Prentice-Hall, 1987), 25.

III. The Imperfect Art

1. Nat Shapiro and Nat Hentoff, *Hear Me Talkin' to Ya'.* (New York: Rinehart, 1955), 93.
2. *Downbeat,* May 18, 1978, 42.
3. Albert Lord, *The Singer of Tales* (Cambridge: Harvard Univ. Press, 1960).
4. Quoted in John Rockwell's *All American Music* (New York: Alfred A. Knopf, 1983), 166.
5. Alan Lomax, *Mr. Jelly Roll* (Berkeley: Univ. of California Press, 1950), 60.
6. Donald Marquis, *In Search of Buddy Bolden* (New York: Da Capo Press, 1978), 102.
7. Lomax, *Mr. Jelly Roll,* 60.

8. *Ibid.*

9. Marshall Stearns, *The Story of Jazz* (New York: Oxford Univ. Press, 1956), 224–25.

10. From the liner notes to Miles Davis's *Kind of Blue* (Columbia PC 8163).

11. James Collier, *The Making of Jazz* (New York: Granada Publishing Ltd., 1978), 72.

12. Richard Sudhalter and Philip Evans, *Bix: Man and Legend* (London: Quartet Books, 1974), 35–39.

IV. Neoclassicism in Jazz

1. Cited in J. C. Thomas, *Chasin' the Trane* (New York: Doubleday, 1975), 132.

2. Gunther Schuller, *Early Jazz* (New York: Oxford Univ. Press, 1968), 146.

3. Alan Lomax, *Mr. Jelly Roll* (Berkeley, Univ. of California Press, 1950), 63.

4. *Ibid.*

5. J. C. Thomas, *Chasin' the Trane* (New York: Doubleday, 1975), 109.

6. *Ibid.*, 90.

7. Philip Larkin, *All What Jazz* (New York: Farrar, Straus & Giroux, 1985), 21.

8. Pauline Rivelli and Robert Levin, eds., *Black Giants* (New York: World Publishing, 1970).

9. This and below quoted in *Jazz Times,* Feb. 1982. See also *Downbeat,* April 1982, p. 12.

10. William Thrall, *A Handbook to Literature* (New York: Odyssey Press, 1960), 431.

11. M. H. Abrams, *The Mirror and the Lamp: Romantic Theory and the Critical Tradition* (New York: Oxford Univ. Press, 1953), 94.

12. Cited in *ibid.*, 93.

13. *Downbeat,* Sept. 15, 1960, p. 17.

14. *Ibid.*

15. It appeared in *Punch* on Jan. 10, 1973.

16. Nat Hentoff, *Village Voice,* Aug. 22, 1977.

17. *Downbeat,* Oct. 16, 1958, p. 43.

18. *Downbeat,* Sept. 15, 1960, p. 37.

19. *Ibid.,* 16.

20. Oswald Spengler, *The Decline of the West,* trans., Charles Francis Atkinson (New York: Alfred A. Knopf, 1928), 245.

21. *Ibid.,* 238.

22. *Ibid.,* 237.

23. Quoted in *Downbeat,* March 25, 1976.

24. Edgar Wind, *Art and Anarchy* (New York: Alfred A. Knopf, 1963), 28.

V. What Has Jazz to Do with Aesthetics?

1. Cyril Barrett, ed., *L. Wittgenstein: Lectures and Conversations on Aesthetics, Psychology, and Religious Belief, Compiled from Notes Taken by Yorick Symthies, Rush Rees, and James Taylor* (Oxford: Basil Blackwell, 1966), 11.

2. Carl Dalhaus, *Esthetics of Music* (New York: Cambridge Univ. Press, 1981). For a broader discussion of the view of activity as a defining element in culture see Johan Huizinga's seminal study *Homo Ludens: A Study of the Play-element in Culture* (Boston: Beacon Press, 1955).

3. Nelson Goodman, *Languages of Art* (New York: Bobbs-Merrill, 1968).

4. Eduard Hanslick, *The Beautiful in Music* (New York: Liberal Arts Press, 1957), 97. For Kant's views see *The Critique of Judgement* (New York: Hafner Publishing, 1966), 173–75.

5. Georg Lukacs, *History and Class Consciousness* (Cambridge, Mass.: MIT Press, 1971), esp. 83–110.

6. John Dewey, *Art as Experience* (New York: Capricorn Books, 1958), 3.

7. Benedetto Croce, *Aesthetic: As Science of Expression and General Linguistic* (New York: Macmillan, 1922).

8. Arthur C. Danto, *The State of the Art* (New York: Prentice-Hall, 1987), 59. See also Deborah Solomon, *Jackson Pollock* (New York: Simon and Schuster, 1987) 178–82.

9. Hermann Weyl, *Symmetry* (Princeton: Princeton Univ. Press, 1952), 3.
10. Umberto Eco, *Art and Beauty in the Middle Ages,* trans., Hugh Bredin (New Haven: Yale Univ. Press, 1986), 40.
11. Frederick Turner, *Natural Classicism* (New York: Paragon, 1985).

VI. *Boredom and Jazz*

1. Gary Giddins, *Celebrating Bird* (New York: William Morrow, 1987), 66.
2. E. E. Evans-Pritchard, ed., *The Institutions of Primitive Society* (Glencoe, Ill.: The Free Press, 1954), 32.
3. Frederick Turner, *Natural Classicism* (New York: Paragon, 1985), 251.
4. Leonard Meyer, *Emotion and Meaning in Music* (Chicago: Univ. of Chicago Press, 1956).
5. Cited in Ira Gitler's *Jazz Masters of the Forties* (New York: Macmillan, 1966), 246.
6. Cited in Giddins, *Celebrating Bird,* 56.
7. "Minimal Abstracts," from *Minimal Art: A Critical Anthology,* ed., Gregory Battock (New York: E. P. Dutton, 1968), 260.

VII. *Jazz as Song*

1. Albert Lord, *The Singer of Tales* (Cambridge: Harvard Univ. Press, 1960), 42.
2. Quoted in Robert Reiner, *Bird: The Legend of Charlie Parker* (New York: Citadel, 1962), 152.
3. Billie Holiday, *Lady Sings the Blues* (New York: Lancer Books, 1965), 50.
4. John McDonough, "The Court Martial of Lester Young," *Downbeat,* Jan. 1981, pp. 18–19.
5. See Lewis Porter's *Lester Young* (Boston: Twayne Publishers, 1985), 26.
6. *Ibid.,* 15.

7. Quoted in Nat Hentoff, *The Jazz Makers* (New York: Grove Press, 1957), 249.
8. Porter, *Lester Young*, 29.
9. Holiday, *Lady Sings the Blues*, 59.
10. Whitney Balliett, *American Singers* (New York: Oxford Univ. Press, 1979), 75.
11. *Ibid.*

INDEX

Abrams, M. H., 82
Abstract expressionism, 104–105, 131
Allen, Henry "Red," 65
Ansermet, Ernst-Alexandre, 24
Antheil, George, 12
Apollinaire, Guillaume, 26–28
Archipenko, A. P., 26–27
Arlen, Harold, 110, 139
Armstrong, Louis, 3–8, 11, 15–18, 19–20, 28–30, 36, 42, 51, 65, 67, 70–71, 73, 77, 82, 83, 84, 93, 110, 123, 133, 139, 140
Art and Anarchy (Wind), 93
Art and Beauty in the Middle Ages (Eco), 106
Austen, Jane, 86
Aux Frontieres du Jazz (Goffin), 28

Bach, J. S., 54, 99, 101, 114
Bailey, William "Buster," 64
Baker, Chet, 87, 90, 139
Ballet mecanique (Antheil), 12
Balliett, Whitney, 17, 40, 80, 123, 139
Banks, Joseph, 20
Barthes, Roland, 114, 125–126
Bartók, Bela, 71–72
Basie, William "Count," 5, 34, 85, 116, 117, 134, 136, 137
Beatles, 14
Beattie, Ann, 121
"Beauty" (Coleman), 40
Bechet, Sidney, 23–24, 25, 34, 51, 133
Beethoven, Ludwig van, 12, 54, 67, 92
Beiderbecke, Leon "Bix," 5, 64–65, 71, 112, 139
Benjamin, Walter, 3, 10, 11
Bennett, Tony, 139
Berlin, Irving, 139
Berman, Lazar, 9
Bernini, Giovanni, 104
Bernstein, Leonard, 41

Berry, Leon "Chu," 34
Bigard, Barney, 34
Blackwell, Ed, 39
Blakey, Art, 79
Blanton, Jimmy, 44
Blesh, Rudi, 35–36
Bley, Paul, 41–42
"Bloomdido" (Parker), 131
"Blues (Fast)" (Parker), 131
Bolden, Charles "Buddy," 56–57, 71, 134
Bostic, Earl, 78
Botticelli, Sandro, 91
Bradford, Bobby, 39
Brown, Clifford, 72
Brubeck, Dave, 86–88
Brubeck, Michael, 90
Bryant, Ray, 52–53
Brymm, Tim, 23
Byron, Lord George Gordon, 82

Capote, Truman, 61
Carey, Dave, 26
Carter, Benny, 71
Carter, Elliott, 54
Carver, Raymond, 121
Cellini, Benvenuto, 106
"Cherokee" (Noble), 57, 118–119
Cherry, Don, 37, 39–42
Chevalier, Maurice, 24
Chopin, Frederic, 9
Christian, Charlie, 115
Clarke, Kenny, 115
Clay, James, 39
Cole, Bill, 31–32
Cole, Nat, 139
Coleman, Ornette, 37–44, 123, 133, 140
Collier, James Lincoln, 24, 37, 42, 64
Coltrane, Alice, 81
Coltrane, John, 31–32, 58, 71, 72, 77, 78–81, 82, 83, 133
Combelle, Alix, 20
Confrey, Zez, 25
Connors, Red, 38

"Construction Gang" (Edwards), 77
Cook, James, 20
Cook, Will Marion, 23
"La Creation du Monde" (Milhaud), 22
Croce, Benedetto, 103
Crosby, Bing, 139
Cubism, 131
Cunningham, Bradley, 90

Dalhaus, Carl, 98
Dali, Salvador, 52
Dameron, Tadd, 110
Danto, Arthur, 46
Davis, Anthony, 123
Davis, Miles, 42, 61, 73, 78, 79, 80, 85, 133
Decline of the West, The (Spengler), 91–92
Deconstruction, 67
"The Dehumanization of Art" (Ortega y Gasset), 11
Delaunay, Charles, 25–29
Delaunay, Robert, 26–27
Delaunay-Terk, Sonia, 26
DeMichaels, Don, 40
"Des Canniballes" (Montaigne), 21
"Des Coches" (Montaigne), 21
Desmond, Paul, 85, 86–91, 92
Dewey, John, 100
Diderot, Denis, 21
"Dippermouth Blues" (Oliver), 132
Dodds, Johnny, 34–36
Dusen, Frankie, 57
Dylan, Bob, 136

Early Jazz (Schuller), 75
East India Company, 20
"The Easy Winners" (Joplin), 75
Eckstine, Billy, 118, 139
Eco, Umberto, 106
Edison, Thomas, 8, 63–66
Eliot, T. S., 52, 62
Ellington, Edward Kennedy "Duke," 5, 25, 28–29, 65, 73, 76, 80, 84, 93, 110, 112–113, 134, 139
"Embraceable You" (Gershwin), 60

Emotion and Meaning in Music (Meyer), 113–114
Encyclopedia of Jazz (Feather), 24
Europe, James Reese, 22
Evans, Bill, 40, 61, 72, 85, 110, 133
Evans, Gil, 93
Evans, Herschel, 116

Faerie Queen (Spenser), 107
Feather, Leonard, 24
Fellini, Federico, 13, 52
Feyerabend, Paul, 73
Fina, Jack, 87
Foster, George "Pops," 33, 36
Fra Angelico, 96
Freudian theories of art, 67
"Furniture Music" (Satie), 10–11

Gardner, Goon, 118
Garner, Erroll, 33
George V, King of England, 23
Gershwin, George, 4, 110, 139
Getz, Stan, 85, 127, 133
Giacometti, Alberto, 46
"Giant Steps" (Coltrane), 58, 80
Giddins, Gary, 44, 111
Gillespie, John Birks "Dizzy," 57, 78, 93, 114, 115, 119–120
Giuffre, Jimmy, 40
Glass, Philip, 12, 121
Goethe, Johann Wolfgang van, 82
Goffin, Robert, 25, 27–32, 47
Goodman, Benny, 136
Goodman, Nelson, 99
Gordon, Dexter, 140
Gothic art, 68
Gould, Glenn, 14, 129
Granz, Norman, 120, 135
"Guernica" (Picasso), 62

Hadlock, Richard, 6, 29
Hammond, John, 136
Hanslick, Eduard, 99
Haqq, Ramakrishna King, 81
Hardin, Lil, 34, 51
Harmolodics, 43–44
Hartman, Johnny, 80
Hawkesworth, John, 20–21

Hawkins, Coleman, 34, 65, 79, 133, 136–137
Haydn, Franz Joseph, 92
Haymes, Dick, 138
Haywood, William, 22
Hegel, Georg, 115
Heidegger, Martin, 11, 70
Hellfighters, 22–23
Henderson, Fletcher, 5–6, 25, 29, 34, 137
Henderson, Leora, 137
Hentoff, Nat, 41, 88
Higgins, Billy, 39–40
Hindemith, Paul, 71–72
Hines, Earl, 34, 112, 119
Hitchcock, Alfred, 52
Hodges, Johnny, 71, 78
Holiday, Billie, 85, 134, 136, 137
Hollenberg, David, 52–53
Homer, 53, 130
Hoover, Herbert, 65
Horn of Plenty (Goffin), 28
Horowitz, Vladimir, 129
Hot Jazz (Panassie), 25
Hot Discography (Delaunay), 25–26
Howard, John Tasker, 24–25
Hulme, T. E., 14–15
Hume, David, 115
"The Hymn" (Parker), 86

"I've Got Rhythm" (Gershwin), 57, 110

Jackson, Michael, 73
Jackson, Tony, 34
Jarrett, Keith, 59
Jazz Directory (Carey & McCarthy), 26
Jazz: From the Congo to the Metropolitan (Goffin), 28, 30
Jazz Hot, Le, 32
Jazz, Hot and Hybrid (Sargeant), 32–33
Johnson, William "Bunk," 23
Johnson, James P., 34
Johnson, Samuel, 115
Jones, David, 36
Jones, Elvin, 31–32
Jones, Jo, 117

Joplin, Scott, 25, 34, 75
Joyce, James, 62
"Just Friends" (Lewis/Klenner) 72

Kant, Immanuel, 99, 125
Keats, John, 82
Keppard, Freddie, 23
Kern, Jerome, 139
Kerouac, Jack, 61
Keyes, Lawrence, 116
Kierkegaard, Søren, 10
Kind of Blue (Davis), 61, 79
Kirk, Andy, 116
"Klactoveedsedstene" (Parker), 42
Klee, Paul, 46
Koenig, Les, 39–40
Kofsky, Frank, 81
"KoKo" (Parker), 86
Konitz, Lee, 89
Krasner, Lee, 104
Kuhn, Thomas, 73
Kyd, Thomas, 127

Lady Sings the Blues (Holiday), 134
Langridge, Derek, 29
Larkin, Philip, 80–81, 115
Lauper, Cyndi, 73
Leach, Edmund, 112
Le Corbusier, Charles-Edouard, 62
Lee, George, 117
Lewis, John, 40–41, 85, 93
Lewis, Ted, 25
Lippi, Filippino, 91
Liszt, Franz, 9
Live (Desmond), 90
Lomax, Alan, 75
Lord, Albert, 53, 130
"Love for Sale" (Porter), 110
Lukacs, Georg, 11, 99–100
Lunceford, Jimmie, 5

Macero, Teo, 79
Making of Jazz, The (Collier), 37
"Manha de Carnival" (Bonfa), 90
Marsalis, Wynton, 72, 73
Marxism, 67, 99–100
Matisse, Henri, 52
McCarthy, Albert, 26
McShann, Jay, 116, 119

"Merry-Go-Round" (Parker), 131
Meyer, Leonard, 113–114
Michelangelo Buonarroti, 91
Milhaud, Darius, 22, 88
Mingus, Charles, 56, 83, 110, 131
Minimalism, 12, 113, 121–122, 124
Mitchell, George, 76
Mitchell, Keith "Red," 39
Modern Jazz Quartet, 40
Modigliani, Amedeo, 45
Mondrian, Piet, 121
Monk, Thelonious, 56, 78, 79, 83,
    110, 115, 133
Monk's Music (Monk), 79
Montaigne, Michel Eyquem de, 21
Montgomery, Wes, 85
"Moose the Mooche" (Parker), 120
Morton, Ferdinand "Jelly Roll," 16,
    33, 50–51, 56–57, 75–76, 77, 93,
    110, 112, 140
Moses, Grandma, 43
Mozart, Wolfgang, 54, 67, 92,
    102, 104
"Muggles" (Armstrong), 7
Mulligan, Gerry, 87
Muzak, 11

New Age music, 122–123
Nietzsche, Friedrich, 10, 91
"Night in Tunisia" (Gillespie), 120
Noone, Jimmy, 34
Norris, Walter, 39–40
Novalis, 83

Odyssey (Homer), 130
Oliver, Joe "King," 3–6, 23, 51, 76,
    93, 110, 112, 129, 132–133, 134
On the Road (Kerouac), 61
Orchestra Rehearsal (Fellini), 13
Original Dixieland Jass Band, 64
"Ornithology" (Parker), 120
Ortega y Gasset, José, 11–12, 14,
    15, 16
Ory, Kid, 35
Our American Music (Howard),
    24–25
"Over the Rainbow" (Arlen), 110

Paganini, Niccolò, 9

Panassie, Hugues, 19–21, 25, 28–
    30, 32–33
Parker, Charlie, 25, 38, 41, 56, 57,
    60, 65, 67, 71–72, 79, 83, 84,
    86–87, 93, 114, 115–121, 122,
    123, 129, 130–131, 133
Parker, Pree, 72
Parker, Rebecca, 117
Payne, Don, 39–40
Pepper, Art, 72
Perreault, John, 124
Peterson, Oscar, 72
Picasso, Pablo, 45, 62
Picou, Alphonse, 34–35
Plato, 10, 100
Pleasants, Henry, 115
Pollock, Jackson, 103–105
Pop Art, 131
Porter, Cole, 110, 139
"Potato Head Blues" (Armstrong),
    7, 77
Pound, Ezra, 7, 62
Powell, Earl "Bud," 38, 57, 114,
    115, 136
"Prime Time for Harmolodics"
    (Coleman), 43
Priscus, 21
Proust, Marcel, 62, 122

Ramey, Gene, 117
Ravel, Maurice, 22
Real Jazz, The (Panassie), 25,
    29–30
Redman, Don, 34, 112
Reich, Steve, 12, 121
Reid, Daniel, 22
Reification, 99–100
Rembrandt van Rijn, 96
Remembrance of Things Past
    (Proust), 62
Rey, Alvino, 87
"Rhapsody in Blue" (Gershwin),
    4, 51
Roach, Max, 40, 115
Robichaux, John, 34
Robinson, Bill "Bojangles," 22
Rodgers, Richard, 139
Romanticism, 81–83
Roosevelt, Franklin D., 134
Rothko, Mark, 121

Rousseau, Jean-Jacques, 21
Rushing, Jimmy, 116
Ruskin, John, 44–45, 68
Russell, Ross, 120

Sargeant, Winthrop, 32–33
Satchmo (Armstrong), 36
Satie, Erik, 10–11
Schuller, Gunther, 8, 40, 75
"The Second Coming" (Yeats), 92
Shakespeare, William, 102, 127
"Shanghai Shuffle" (Armstrong), 6
Shank, Clifford "Bud," 89
"She Rote" (Parker), 131
Shearing, George, 38
"Shoe Shine Boy" (Cahn/
  Chaplin), 134
"Sidewalk Blues" (Morton), 76
Simeon, Omar, 34, 76
Sinatra, Frank, 138, 139
Singer of Tales, The (Lord), 53,
  130
Singleton, Zutty, 34
Sleep (Warhol), 121–122
Smith, Al, 4
Smith, Bessie, 25
Smith, Henry "Buster," 118
Smith, Joe, 5
Smith, Willie, 34
Socrates, 123
Solo Concerts (Jarrett), 59
Something Else! (Coleman), 40–41
Sontag, Susan, 123
Southern Syncopated Orchestra, 23
Spengler, Oswald, 91–92
Spenser, Edmund, 107
Springsteen, Bruce, 136
Squier, George Owen, 11
Stafford, Jo, 138
Stern, Chip, 44
Stewart, Rex, 6
Storyville, 34
Stravinsky, Igor, 71, 122
"Struttin' with Some Barbeque"
  (Armstrong), 7

Tacuma, Jamaaladeen, 44
"Take Five," 89
Tate, George "Buddy," 116
Tatum, Art, 34, 118

Taylor, Cecil, 140
Thompson, Virgil, 25
Thrall, William, 82
Tio, Lorenzo, 34–35
350th Artillery Band, 23
Torme, Mel, 139
Tough, Dave, 58
Tourneur, Cyril, 127
Treat It Gentle (Bechet), 23
Tristano, Lennie, 58, 116
Trumbauer, Frankie, 65
Turner, Frederick, 107, 113
Tynan, John, 41

Ulanov, Barry, 28
Ulmer, James, 43

Vallee, Rudy, 116
Varese, Edgar, 72
Vinci, Leonardo da, 91–92, 97, 106
Vinson, Eddie "Cleanhead," 78
Vodery, Will, 23
Vriesen, Gustav, 26

Wagner, Richard, 11, 82
Waller, Thomas "Fats," 34, 139
Warhol, Andy, 108, 121–122
Waters, Ethel, 5
"Wave" (Jobim), 90
Webster, Ben, 116
"Wendy" (Desmond), 90
"West End Blues" (Armstrong), 7,
  16, 83
Weyl, Hermann, 105
Whiteman, Paul, 4, 5, 25, 28
Williams, Martin, 41, 92
Williams, Mary Lou, 116
Wilson, John, 80
Wind, Edgar, 93–94
Wittgenstein, Ludwig, 95, 97
Wolf, Hugo, 128
World War I, 22–23
Wordsworth, William, 82

"Yardbird Suite" (Parker), 120
Yeats, William Butler, 92
"You Go to My Head" (Coots/
  Gillespie), 87
Young, Lester, 44, 56, 65, 71, 85,
  116, 117, 123, 127, 133–138,
  140